LONGING

GIULIA DE GREGORIO LISTO

ISBN: 9781077701137

WE ALL HAVE A VOID INSIDE US.
WHAT MATTERS IS HOW WE FILL IT.
WHAT DO YOU LONG FOR?

CONTENTS

ACKNOWLEDGMENTS

There were times when writing this book felt impossible. The organic flow of poetry seemed to get lost in the untameable ocean of words needed to compose this work.

But I have been showered with love and encouragement that turned shards of me into a complete being.

I want to thank my family and beloved ones for understanding my absences, my anxiety (that grew with every page), and my need to retreat to either write, edit or just think.

I would never have conceived "Longing" if it wasn't for the love, support, advice, care and understanding of those around me.

I want to thank my editor, Anna Rozwadowska, who had the patience and mastery to advise me on the best way to phrase the pieces, the best routes to clarify my often-crazy thoughts, helping to improve the overall quality of this book.

I want also to dedicate this book to the memory of one of my biggest inspirations, Sylvia Plath, who has been my muse, making me believe that, indeed, everything in life is writable about, you only need the guts to do so.

My thank you as well to the Medium Community who has made me trust my poetical abilities and that I should be here, doing this, unafraid and unapologetically.

INTRO

There is always something missing...

I've scavenged dictionaries, feelings and wounds, sticking my finger deep into the pain, trying to find a name for it.

It seemed easier having a title, a way to invoke and expel the void that was installed in my heart right after birth - or perhaps before.

Whenever I found a name and thought I was rid of it, whenever I believed to be fulfilled, change would invade my veins, and my myopic eyes would forget colours and shapes, setting me off into learning the world again.

Walking around with a relentless gap made me a hungry black hole, consuming the universe in my attempts to catalogue myself.

Longing came hurrying, a train I could never catch except for a glimpse, the smoke intoxicating my lungs in an addictive way until I was completely devoid of anything concrete, devoted to a ghost of demands.

I braided words in my attempts to swim above the dark, bottomless ocean. A safety net taking me back to a place I could call home, leading me to the lighthouse as a numb moth that takes every gleam for the sun.

Now I share the rope for you to hold on to.

This beacon of light.

This eternal longing.

LONGING

ELUSIVE

Consider all of the things I try to be
Even when I can't.
Consider the words that I speak
Even when I cannot breathe.
Consider my feet, one after the other,
Even when my body is crumbling.
Consider my attempts and my half-conquers,
Consider the mask I wear, and how I structure my way
through life,
Consider the paths I wish to take,
Even when I'm frightened.

Consider my coldness as drywall to not overflow.
Consider the silence I keep in order to listen,
Even when I don't agree.
Consider how my body recovers time after time,
Consider the strength it has to come back,
Consider the life inside me.
Consider all of the things I try to do,
Even when I end up crawling in bed.
Consider my cries and my sighs and my lies
Even when I could just let it all be.

Consider the love I want to give,
Even when I find it easier to close myself off.
Consider who I am and who I want to be,
Even when I'm unsure if I'll get there.

Consider me.

HOLY GRAIN

Nothing has been defined in me
My limbs slowly dismantling
Like stones rolling to the ground; hitting it
With such a violent sound,
Such a resentment

I did not give up
I just have nothing to hold it in place
No stickiness to pretend I'm whole,
So I just watch it fall, stone after stone
Until I cannot walk nor talk nor breathe
Just one pillar, a centred Stonehenge
Made of flesh, still pulsating

But each time, slower,
Each time with fewer dreams
Of standing straight.
I carry the desire of laying down
And sleeping for ages,
Until I become something sacred.
A place people will visit and offer prayers
My torso covered in thick grass
Surrounded by the smaller stones of my fingers
A circular site of attraction; yet
I'm a magical failure

Maybe one day I could wake up,
Clean my scanty body of old litanies,
Sculpt myself back again, into smaller fragments
And wander about the world collecting what has been lost.
Unable to disappoint any more
Because if I give up, if I dismantle again
I'll be gravel that crunches beneath the feet

Of those seeking sacred grounds.
A grain cannot be bothered by pain,
So neither will I.

OUTBREAK

I can feel my thoughts vanishing.

The more I think of it
The more they fly away.
Angry doves in search of a warmer home
Leaving the grey plaster, the chewed up gum that sticks to
their feet.

Just like my thoughts, I seek a type of deliverance
From the retaining fear that holds me, that keeps me in one
place
As I watch things slip with infuriating velocity.

I'm standing on the platform and the train is near but my
pockets are empty; I try
To scour my mind to remind where I lost the tickets,
From which hole they fell and what did I replace them with,
Because the weight is there but the certainty is not,
Not anymore.

These are the mind-wrecking stages of consciousness, I hear
someone say.
The steps that build character by destroying me, string by
string,
As a knitted doll that loses its parts until you cannot
recognize it any longer.
Only the button eyes, lifeless, hanging from a thin line of
events
I wish I had not witnessed.

I'm tied to the pills, they nest on the palm of my hand.
Their pink hue tries to lock my wondering inside,
To set aside any trace of marrow in exchange for pleasant

belonging.
I don't own a title but a name tag, pierced through my breast for everyone
To see and understand.
I own a diagnosed signature, which I bind contracts with.
The trustworthy anchor is blaming me.
The thoughts have escaped; they are running like wild animals,
They are in danger, hosting terrible diseases.

I feel they run all over me, the liberated herd of thinking
That does not stop for something that used to be free,
Because now it is their time to live and I was selfish,
Keeping them all to myself.

THE PAIN THAT LASTS

So many stones have gathered in my pockets
And many more in my hands.

They have titles of their own.
They have rooms of their own inside my chest.

I can feel their contour encompassing my collarbone,
A heavy necklace I've received to never forget
The burden of being the one to animate this skin.

This soul always changing from one thing to another,
Yet boringly the same, driving me mad,
One wrinkle at a time.

The water rises, ankle-deep.
My toes freeze at an alarming speed.
This must be how a caterpillar feels, surrounding
Itself with a constrained cocoon.
I too desire to fly at the end.

A moth searching for a lighthouse or any other
Beacon of light and hope.
But the water seems more pleased in receiving me
Than happiness ever was.
Water opens like the welcoming arms of a mother.
Like returning to the beginning,
Way before things started to curdle.

When my mouth was less insipid,
No ashes covering my tongue,

Only the delightful taste of learning new words.

I feel like a 300-year old woman,
Beyond tired of this place and this life and this land.
My hands won't grow anything further.
My body won't keep anything warm, not even its own bones,
And my mind won't think straight.
It won't braid any more indecorous lines.

I've paid my tolls more than twice
And leaving is well overdue.

My rigid arms should become a boat,
And my legs, the oversized anchor,
Leading me below, to the land of peace.
To this singular but spectacular day,
When I'll be born with the sun,
And set down with the waves.

CLIFFHANGER

This is it, I think. This is it. The utmost sacrifice,
The final step of a chained promise to remain walking.
This is the dark night of it. When you reach the cliff
And it looks back at you, wanting answers. Wanting motion.
I've reached the seams of the map, there's no extra mile
To base myself on. I'm in a midseason of feelings.
My feet have a purifying quality, they erase the path
As I leave it behind; two strong brooms making way
For sanctity that I never possessed.

This is it, me and the high edge of the cliff.
The rocks seem to long for me, their eager stubs as
Gluttonous fingers. *I'm not afraid.* I thought I'd be petrified.
But they seem a much better way to lay down than
Keeping company to the sun, as it raises in a sick yellow tone,
To which I attend, the caretaker, always willing.
Never sleeping.
The bottom seems more secure to me, a mother's lap,
And not the incessant shake of hard winds against my feeble
skin.

There's a sound as if prophecies were told through
interference.
They do not shout, they buzz around and you might kill them
By ignoring their predictions until it's too late.
I've killed them all, a handful of insights I could have
followed
But deemed too hard, too complicated, too much for me.
Why is it that I cannot place myself anywhere monumental
Unless it precedes a fall?
Why can't I occupy the same place,
The same altar I've used to honour others?

So this is it. I'm taking the final steps towards a jump.

For a falling-into-place moment.
This is that important; oblivious day no one never knew existed.
The day things slowly alter into goodbyes.
The day falling down is required to reach other altitudes.
See you soon, cliff-hanging friends.
I was never made for holding on too tightly.

PAMPHLETS

I'm haunted by promises I've made,
By how entangled my life has become.
Commitments I don't want to make with anyone
Because I haven't learned how to give them to myself.
Still, I distribute them as pamphlets
Take one
Take me
I'm here
I'm here
And the promises are still kept, except to myself.

The loud sounds of rage and the cracking of erupted try-outs
take over the room,
Take over the scalding shower I'm under
To wash clean the frozen bites of words
Which were not supposed to be uttered.
Words that should exist only inside the core of the earth,
A voiceless magma for Gaia to transform into fertility

But said, *words are demons*. Guileless,
Inflicting pain without purpose.

If I knew how to take myself more seriously,
Recognize my open wounds as eagerly as I
Recognize others',
Perhaps the pamphlets would become expensive books.
I would handle them out only to those who can afford
To handle me,
With care and mild temperature.

THE BAD SMELL OF THE LIES WE CHOSE TO BELIEVE

There is a painting laughing at me.
Its smile draws music into the empty room,
Nothing else but ink and notes and ashes
From my limbs, burning, exhausted.
It took too long to get here. It was a marathon.

A procession follows on the outside and the room is empty.

They forgot us inside, they are too busy with the candles.
I burn too.
My whole body is a pyre under the eyes of the painting.
Frozen in time, so present, so unlike any other, so alive.
If I could move my knees, I'd bend them.
If I had tears, I'd be a full flowing river.
I'd be salt and ashes and devotion
I'd be a candle in the hands of the procession
So pure and well dressed in wax, in sweat.
I could be the brightest flame she ever stared at.

The golden opulence of her frame
Diminishes me.
I cannot bear another halo swooping her away,
Another pair of wings,
Another homage I could not pay,
My hands so small not even flowers fit,
She left so many times before.

This missing hole inside me
She mocks as she stares
She knows I won't dare say
I won't dare pray for her
Oh, I wouldn't even say her name.
Maybe I'm going insane.

It makes sense we'd fall down
The same pungent coil,
The slow descending.
The bad smell of the lies we chose to believe,
She's the best one.
She has the odour of longing,
Of standing at the porch waiting for the door to open
Of watching an egg hatch,
A seed sprouting.

She smells as the longest delays in life.

And I follow the thin trail of her smoke
Up to the empty room
Up to the still painting made of cold ink
Up to the gas chambers and fireplaces
Up to a pile of promises and poetry just hanging
As bodies on the ceiling.

I'm angry and devastated and undone,
Why did we drag each other to give it another try?
And why do I let you pull me along?

No answers,
Just silence as it has always been.
The same silence you ever gave me
And I burn.
My torso is gone.
My arms are halfway there.
The fingers sinking into the floor.
I burn at the echo of nothing.
Even the fire muffles me
And I go.

Ignored,
Unrequited,
Unsure you were ever here.

THE DOWNFALL

Black skies.
The predators agglutinate as thick clouds.
I cannot look beyond nor grasp a ray of light.

Down here, I've seen people wither.
Limbs becoming frailer and the skin manifesting
A grey, dull aspect.
The complexion of those who have given up, defeated and
hurt.

I feel decrepit, reducing in size and in strength every new day,
Or whatever similar frame could exist without the sun.
The hate waves replace the air and the dome seems to double
With the pressure of abandoned futures.
I want to leave the soil I've been born and raised
Because it no longer nurtures me.

It does not welcome what composes me.

The only dispersion I see comes from the cells of my heart,
Running towards safety without knowing its name.
Collapsing, after so much escape, I drop at the feet of a saint;
Made of old bones and phlegmatic sounds.

I let it rip off me the pain of persisting.
The pain of wanting to live.
My tears baptize me in a feverish broth
And I vocalize prayers in the name of other places,
Where my being would be more than dry sheets of skin,
And I could see the sun again.

AMALGAMATE

I lie down as if old sheets were covering the bed
I feel bleached and purified but empty,
My threads so respectfully intertwined;
Feeling flaccid as beaten skin.
Suddenly the weight you've put on me
Lost resistance against the air

Blindly I raise my hands as a baby in need,
Groaning, turning, searching for you
In the dark,
In the oppressive silence of the room.
My swollen fingers slide down a lock of your hair.

You're an imposing bride carrying a long train.
Even miles away, you're still present.
You're a whole galaxy imploding
Leaving us with the explosions, yet,
There are no stars as I look out the window.

The sky is hepatic as a strange mix of colours
I can't tell it apart from the building in front of me
Maybe all that I'm looking at is concrete
I leave the curtains open for you to come.

Your perfume is of wildflowers and weeds
A hungry breath strolls down my neck
And I know you won't be gone
But you threaten me with distance,
With white cloths and pills to sleep.

You bleed me out and under.
I drip onto newspapers and rejected poems,
What a mess to take off the floor!
You wish you could just ignore the stains,

And the stale smell of life.

You wish you could cut the cord
I wish I could drown in my own fluids
But instead, we hold on
Strong,
Vivid,
A timeless gestation.

I lie down quietly, obediently,
You're a majestic hummingbird,
Opalescent feathers giving the night a gentle breeze,
And the lullabies,
The firm voice,
The melodies you feed me with.
The emptiness is your form of care.
Allowing me to sleep because you know the sun is coming.

You're not leaving,
I'm not a loose thread.
You're nursing the wasted time,
I'm swallowing nostalgia,
We're syncretizing.

BLACK CHAMBER

The windows are open, but I can't breathe.
An anaphylactic kiss;
I succumb to the weight of time,
To the addled paper piling up in the corner of the room,
To the shadow I almost catch seeing.

But then I blink
And I'm alone again.
I feel the currents of air above me,
a tiny trail slips down into my nose,
insufficient and unwilling.
It deflates me,
Night after night.
I give so much more than I take.

The seepage on the wall resembles us.
Water is our element.
The viscosity of my unsustained tears,
The vapour of our brief encounters,
The infiltration of our anger,
The vases collapsing against the plaster,
Casually trickling down to meet the glass and the flowers,
The ebb and flow of time

I kiss you as the waves kiss the shore,
eagerly,
You kiss me as the shore kisses the waves
Goodbye,
Steady and never changing.

The ice-cold truth that won't let me sleep
And the cryogenic dreams,
So slow and stirred together
As the snowballs you'd throw

Amidst our placid wars.

Of all that we could be
We were sea
ocean
rain
smoke
liquor
gas.

We could oscillate
from 50° to 120°
And still take form
And still destroy each other.

Of all elements,
We were water

That is why you're crawling inside my wall
Dark as the depths
That is why I'm constantly thirsty
And no amount of water is ever enough.

DEPRIVATION

In nights like this, one could claim to have found peace.

The halfway-clean house, the tiles open in a path, all ready
and set.
I guess I haven't been sleeping because I end up waiting for
you,
While it would be easier to find you in my dreams.

Three weeks I've been meeting the sun in the mornings,
Saying goodbye to my fantasies as they rush me against the
clock.
I could not find a name for what kept me awake.
Yours was so obvious, I thought I was over wasting nights on
it.

In my rare dreams, I'm always running, always going towards
a place unreachable and I can't remember where.
Whenever I'm close to a memory, they seem to fly back to
the same place you live in.

I live in waiting hours.
Every step I hear teases me, every window I look holds a
promise I don't recall,
but my heart seems sure you'll appear.
Every person could be you if I look attentively enough.
Every movie character could be us and every story could be
ours, too.
Every song could be telling our story—most times that's how
I hear them.
That's the reason why I fall so deeply in love with artwork
You're the piece I've been looking for.

I'm so terribly attracted to people with crazy dreams.
By those trying to reach other worlds.

Perhaps together we could create a portal and intrude upon
another time.
Maybe love was always meant to be a key.

There's not a silent night in the city and I comply.
The loud voice of an angel out of the speakers turns the
longing into the ethereal.
I want to believe it to be pure, I want to believe us to be the
truth,
but in the back of my mind, I have never been sure.

Maybe I've been chasing ghosts and bleached dreams,
because I don't want to call life ordinary.
Maybe my specialty is to find different names for loneliness.
And you've always suited it, perfectly.

VENUS TRAP

I opened as if I've never been hurt.

Legs and arms spread out, so far from each other
One could believe I was dismantled.
And that's how I felt.

A war toddler that forgot all the past trauma.
I've befriended the voices that come out of the gutter.
I trust their advice; the open way that they approach life.

I might be my own haunting.
Faith is a good way to lie and I breathe it in blindly.
Love glitters as a saviour.
The bad dictator people choose to believe in, because sorrow
Stings less than hunger.

Being full of dead flies is still better than the corrosive
emptiness.
The way one's stomach eats itself and demands more.
I have no more to give, so I fashion you. A replica, a placebo
in the sacred name of Love.
If I close my eyes with enough force, I can picture other faces
and smell other scents
The famine can taste grease in their mouths while eating sand.

The war has been over for decades.
Through the windows, you see a world gestated.
Still, my room holds piles of bodies that have not been
Reclaimed.
No families, no loved ones.
They've made my bed their final nest.
Death and I have many mutual friends.

I must warn you, you might be dead before sunrise.

As your side effects diminish and my veins replace every
Ounce of you,
I could just leave the addiction behind and face the hole in
my core alone.

I might discover this spectre never had your face, only an
outline of your being.
The more I push the pieces inside, the more it loses shape,
And I'm left with a twisted affection.
I don't think I ever knew what love actually was supposed to look like.

My rib cage is a Venus trap, chewing my own heart.
The vibrant red nectar attracting others, unaware.
I wish you could read me and perceive my yellow stripes.
All of my venomous signs.

Still, I wish you were brave enough to dare,
Because every deadly being desires to be loved.

FRESHLY PICKED SORROW

Strictly stabbed into the earth, my feet are stuck.
I feel as if I've lost my synchrony with the world,
and I can't get back on the same rhythm
Without losing who I've become.

Like a flower, unwillingly planted onto other land.
The roots grow stronger and I cannot pull them out without killing
Parts of me.
I have a strong core but a fragile exterior; it terrifies me
That I might have to live with the pain of letting my leaves go.

My clockwise petals seem to be moving in another direction.
I'm dizzy. The thoughts and words are in a loud argument
and I'm bothered,
Like my own neighbour, living in the constricted apartment between
The mind and the mouth.
They shout at each other, but I observe through blurry windows.
I'm only sightseeing. A tourist following the daily life of the ordinary.
Then I open my eyes, one day, and the light burns the film.
I can't recall a thing.

My being seems to be down on my knees. They tremble but I hold up.
I might not be able to breathe but I'm standing, I'm pretty to glance at.
I conceal my delay and for everybody else, I'm a sunflower,
Spinning with congruence and desire.
They do not notice how my colour seems faded, how I'm much more thorns

Than I am a flower.
I'm not a fancy Rose in a bouquet, nor an exotic Tulip from
abroad. I do not own the mathematical accuracy of a
Camellia.

I possess the angry qualities of a Carnation.
The mortuary robe of a Chrysanthemum.
Flowers that carry longing in their names,
Flowers you count distances with.
Flowers you selfishly tore apart to discover if someone loves
you.
And my spread remaining blooms into requests…

Forget-me-not.
Forget-me-not
Forget-me-not

EROS & PRAGMA

It has been a hurtful one,
This love.

The way it climbs onto my veins and gnaws at them,
Trying to feed out of my poor reservations that,
So carefully, I've stacked up for times of scarcity.
The way it defies my holiness and interweaves
Between the pedestal and the gutter.

All my life, it feels, I've been preparing for this.

For this rush, for the nights I'm forbidden to sleep,
Trying to figure out how to approach you,
Connecting pieces that reveal themselves to me as a lint of
time,
So battered I'm afraid to touch and see them
Disappear before me, as if never existed.

You got me on a blind faith day.

I converted immediately because you had the same beauty
Of believing in things we cannot reach.
You had eyes, skin, voice and liturgy,
Yet distant enough to keep it unprofane.
I felt as a Hestian virgin when I first saw you,
Consumed by the fire without noticing.
I opened my legs and arms and soul to the flames
Letting it rip off me every trace of sin.
I became immaculate by you.

But it has been a penance.
I'm trying to mend the strings of life.
The Moirai observe me amused as I run after it.
They cast shadows and reflections wondering if I'll ever stop.

They give me new inches of life as a gift for my conviction.
I'm never able to reach the seams to measure how much of your thread
Was recycled onto mine.

The weaver did impeccable work.

I'm still hungry, however, for the nectar you should've given me.
Golden apple trees have risen around you, milk cascading as Hera's sustenance.
But not a single drop left for me to nourish and grow,
To connect me to the mysteries of the world. I'm jostled into another Pantheon
Searching for you amidst a wild syncretism, looking for you in different faces,
In different names, different bodies, different skin tones, different eyes.
Different voices that I may not recognize.
Seeking for the essence, hoping it will answer my prayers.

One day, I'm an Adikian priestess, claiming my unfortunate unfair destiny.
Then, 'I'm a lighten candle for Dike, asking for justice and righteousness.
I'm a descended goddess, rushed down from the skies to receive you
And stabbed, devoid of my sanctity.

Mortality strikes me like lightning.

I roam the city, but I don't know how to live. Therefore, I pray.
I pray to myself. I pray to you. I pray to the remnants of us.
I'm closer to the banished Titans than I was ever close to you.
It is more familiar to me to ride the naked back of Cerberus,

than the stroke of your skin against mine.
The shrieks of Hades are more harmonious to my ears than your voice,
Fading from old tapes, addled in dusty archives.

As Nyx takes the world, so I lay down to let you go.
For one more night, tired and hoarse from my vigil.
The candles go out with a single snuff, the last reservoir of air,
And in my mind, the echoes of your epithets shake the walls,
As if we're at the dawn of the Dardanus.

DILUTED

It seems I'm melting, my brain liquefying,
Running down my spine, making me shiver as a line of cold water.
My shoulders are heavy stones at the margins of this river
That instead of meeting the ocean, is consumed by the ground.
A thirsty earth drinks me whole and I feel as if my being
Is trickling down so fast I cannot reach it, cannot bring myself up again.

Strenuous days heap the walls with new tally marks.
Counting and counting and counting but no idea what for.
I've been waiting with such intensity for something I cannot recognize.
Maybe it is already here, maybe it has arrived and I don't even know.
There's an uncomfortable expectation. I'm lurking on myself, spying through
The windows of my own eyes, trying to locate from where my content
Has been escaping, to separate me from the hoard of others.

But I've been diluted by tears, in showers, in distances.
Dripping along the way and evaporating,
Never really knowing if I lost or if I purified.
Just diluted and twirling as a tiny fish in a current.
I cannot swim against it but I cannot follow it.
Down below, the beasts are waiting
With dark eyes and open mouths.

III. THE EMPRESS

From deaf wall to deaf wall my voice finds no home.
I speak the old language of love and there's no dictionary
Nor tongue to translate what I've been trying to say.

I thought I had lost my tone, maybe I've been stuck in a
dream,
And my attempts to shriek result in nothing more than a
mutter,
A muffled whisper into an old pillow that shares no answers.

Inside my mind, thousands of bridges seemed to carry out the
right purpose,
But I found blockages at the end of the roads and I could not
get to others.
Not through love, not through calmness. Only through the
raging insistence of a tornado, unsympathetic to the effort I
had put in, building stone after stone into
A palace, a fort, a safe house.

There must be something wrong with the acoustics because
the words I say
Echo in different ways. My speech is my own gaslight,
coming out and coming back completely transformed, a
mutation I don't recognize but that carries out my DNA.

Should I be a gentle mother to the monster people made out
of me?

Infinite promises leave my mouth and are received as daggers.

I've learned to see wounds as promises of others I probably
mistook as well.
I've learned that the deeper the wound, the more they wanted
to show me love.

But my love glossary does not find many translators.

I'm in a fright I might be
Completely erased from history, the Valley of the Gods'
unsearched tomb,
The one that holds a mystery no one dares to explore,
perhaps, because
They fear I hold no treasure.

Perhaps they fear I have treasures uncarriable.

Either way, I'm not aware of my place on this ancient map,
My body the conundrum of beauty and existence altogether.
I've seen foreigners ask me questions in multiple idioms, they
want to be
Saved, they're searching through a multitude of faiths for the
right
Goddess of Love and I have so much to share, spells that roll
out of my tongue,
Blessings cascade.

If only they understood my Language.
These ancient inscriptions of Love.

DREAMS ARE PAID FOR

Locked by obligations I cannot bend,
I make my way home, head down and eyes full of tears.
The stream that runs through me wants an explanation better
Than rules and regulation.
It wants a plausible obstacle to rage against.
But all I have to offer is the incapacity.
The small, annoying pins that prick us,
The paper cuts from useless forms we fill,
And how they weigh us
Down and down and down until we're motionless.
Static.
Still.

We boast about having wings but what's the good in that,
If only a few can afford the flight?
I am a stranded ship, sending out help signals but my
telegraph is rusty and obsolete.
Nothing I send out is delivered the same way, only a glitch in
the system.
To the passing-by fleet, I'm exactly where I want to be.
They see me as if intentionally moored.
Some even envy me as if I've landed perfectly at the treasure
chest.
I solely wave my sails and hope that someone realizes I need
to be towed away.

The walk back to reality after a dream collapses is
acrimonious.
It's like chewing sandpaper until your teeth are raw to remind
you not to bite
More than you can fit in the size of your mouth.
Dreams need to be well-measured.
The bigger the dream, the more of your reality you'll sacrifice
for it,

To become something else.

Otherwise, you're given a dark room, reveries at hand for you
to use, to wear,
To stretch, to make yours until the sun comes out again.

You choose the toll, but either way, you'll have to pay.
Not even the dead cross the river for free.

SUSPENSION

I want suspension.
To blink blankly,
To discover myself on the outside
Without time or any concept,
Any kind of mathematical knowledge
That testifies I'm alive.

I want suspension.
An absence of everything,
Without the possibility of longing,
Without knowing what I might be missing.
The heavy door of a lift shutting
And blocking out the sounds,
The lights,
Even time…
But just for two floors
Provoking me into wanting more
Of nothing.

A bee twisting and twirling, eyeless,
Unaware there ever was a hive
Or an egg to begin with.
Unaware there's an endless task,
Unaware honey is even a thing.
Only concerned about flying
And staying off the ground.

Hung in oblivion
That does not taste like forgetting at all.
Just the taste of not existing,
Of stopping,
Without alarms.
Without deadlines.
Without saying a word.

At least until a piece or two falls into place.
Until I blink once more to reveal back the world,
To put it all back into motion.
But for a moment,
Let me not exist at all,
In utter suspension.

IN LIFE'S HANDS

Waiting feels like open-heart surgery.

Trustingly tearing a wound apart to the new things to come,
Pulling my chest open with my bare hands, in deliverance,
Because I want more from life.

I go to sleep as someone who's diving into the unknown.

Every rising sun is a promise, whispers I hear from
coadjutants in my dreams.
I hang on to hope,
I read dreams out loud in this constant waiting room,
Waiting for life to call me, to share the good news.
To say I have been cured of this wanting
And now is the time to be alive.
I survived the test of endurance.

But those are all dreams.

Dreams I've cared for,
And for so long, that I don't know how close I am of
achieving them.
I fear one day I'll wake up, decades from now, and realize I've
only been dreaming, not doing

Creating spaces in my head to fill what was hurting.

Crafting mirrored halls to see other reflections,
Until I forgot which one I was and which one I wanted to be.

I fear life won't call me, my name mixed into a pile of boxes,
And all my waiting will be for nothing.

I would discover myself a storyteller of my own story.

So good at imagining other places and possibilities
But not moving, at all, anywhere

All my energy given to characters I have never been,
Living in places I have never seen.
My whole body languishing, except for the vocal cords,
And the brain, large and heavy from reaching another
Universe.

Still, trust is my biggest sin.

I lay on the cold table, no anaesthesia, no numbness,
Only hoping life isn't trembling as much as I.
My heart wide open, exposed as evidence that I'm ready
To be much more than I am.
I count my beats because I want to impress life,
To pass the test of waiting patiently, resiliently.
Flowing gently as every water stream does,
To reach for higher ground.

REPLACING PAINS

I don't know when I woke up to become an ocean,
But I do know that I've been wavering every feeling,
Every thought, every word.

There are no stories inside me anymore, but a cycle,
A twirled string that, just by a few millimetres,
Does not tie itself
Into a knot.

It feels like I'm going above the speed limit into an obstacle
course.

My foot a lead frame, almost impossible to move,
Smashing the gas pedal and the car floor into a paper-thin
sheet.
I'm feeling everything at once and then nothing.

I can never find the free lane, I can never run with the wind,
Because some impenetrable wall holds me back.
I cannot speed through it, neither can I ignore it.
Nor can I get past its sad, grey tones, its clouded bricks
Standing in my way.

It is more exhausting to feel things in small bits than in
gallons.

To recover only to be covered again in turbulent waters,
Than letting yourself drown at once.
To move at a slow pace using every ounce of breath,
Instead of giving your best to win the marathon and never
looking back.

I rest myself with the anger of not knowing how to be constant.

Something was set free and released my instability.

Like a ferocious animal walking through my veins.

Biting whenever it feels hungry or angry or threatened.
My flesh is full of hollow spaces that I don't know how to fill,
So I rip out sections from other places in my body
From my leaver, my tights, my neck, my back,
Replacing pains and aches with similar ones; only relocated;
Yet different enough to feel as something entertaining.

THIS CITY KILLED MY SANITY

This city killed my sanity,
Every small bit remaining.

I've crossed so many ropes of concrete,
And I don't know if I'm afraid to fall or to complete it.

I lost my bravery with every dark corner I crossed,
Unsure how disfigured I'd appear on the other side,
And how many traumas I'd endure; a morbid collection in my purse,
Stewing before the next green light.

This city killed the person I thought I'd be.

And the friends I thought I'd have.

When they started to convulse in words of hate,
While the foam of their rot mixed with the cold beer
Both overflown,
Killing the warmth of summer in their own way.

The skies of carbon monoxide and fear
Seem to collapse like fragile jaws,
And the acid clings to my skin and muscles and bones,
The fizzing reminds me of past conversations.

Of news I've read on the paper weeks before.
Maybe the reason I've been in so much pain
It's because I've been eating myself from the inside,
Out of mercy.
Out of love for the one I could still turn out to be,
something,
If only the environment wasn't as poisonous

And treacherous.

But this city killed me.

My skin lies on ashtrays and garbage bins
Scattered all over for everyone to see.
A few pay condolences,
Take two seconds of silence
Before their mobiles relieve them of the scenery,
Back to real life. To survival.

For them to succeed where I've fallen.
I hope they do.

TO BE DIVINE AGAIN

This is not what I want,
Chiselled through events and life
And mere portraits of what has been.
I used to be colossal.
Make thunderous sounds,
Leave valleys instead of footprints,
Rivers were my sweet saliva.

The metallic blades of life removed slices of me.
My tongue has a fever,
It cannot stop talking
And complaining
And screaming
And refuting.
It doesn't want to be diminished.

My words acquired an iron taste
And an ironic tone.
I might break the sculptor's arms
And clean my teeth with the nibs of it
Because I don't want to be any smaller,
Any more divided.
I don't want to lose more of myself,
I don't want to leave myself as crumbs,
This is not a path I'm leading.

I'm barely anywhere at all.

This is not what I want,
To be cut as a carton doll
Trying to stay whole while life jostles me
Into the greasy fingers of a child
That has no respect for things
Because it does not understand how

Feeble they can be.

I want to cover the sun.
My body to cause eclipses and never revert
To the same size.
I want to be divine again and
To proclaim how air should behave
Inside each pair of lungs,
So I could find some synchrony.
Some explanation.
I want a gigantic mouth and my voice to
Raise volcanoes from the land,
And to remain intact
For once
Before the chaos of life.

IF TIME ALLOWED US

What an eerie hunt
Going after you, through ages
Time goes by and I'm looking.

You're not here, not geographically,
Not physically,
Not at all.

Yet I cringe every time
As if you were staring at me,
With that blasé glance
With that condescending nod.

What a villainess you are!
I am!
Aren't we too fond of this?

The scratching burns
Where you'd pierce your nails,
Laughing as you chant words,
As you vow to remain
Anchored.
I'm at your feet, at the gold dust
of your hair.

No. You're not here.

My vision shakes,
Time aches,
It only goes forward.
We never reach the same point.
History's invariable,
I missed the race,
The rampant chance

Of belonging to the same place
And the very same space.

Then there's the truth.

The annihilating truth,
That makes one sick,
That makes this all just delusional.

You're over my shoulder.
Cigarette smokes rolling into my hair.
I love and I hate your breath,
Your perfume is stained everywhere.
But we'd entertain one another,
Every time boredom got to us,
Whenever we're too tired to judge,
To criticize all over
And back again.

I dare say we'd be friends.
I would not let you get away.
Not this time.
Not again.

There'd be notes on receipts
You brought from the market,
Only to be seen two weeks later-
No apologies.

I wouldn't even expect it.

But a smile.

Perhaps before you take a shower,
As you convey your emotions to the mirror,
And you'd know that

Finally,
Someone's willing to give it back.

HYSTERICAL STATE OF GRACE

This is who I am without you.

Long lasting.

An internal bleeding of external feelings,
Coagulating inside me. Each clot a word or a phrase.
My blood like curdled milk,
Bubbling and multiplying my anxiety
To break down wall after wall until I reach you.
But afterwards, I shut down as a city under siege, hiding from my own eyes,
Shattering glasses and mirrors that might reflect me, because I don't want
To think about who I am and about what I lack.

I don't think there's a cure for absence.

The splinter develops into a fester, a purulent fear that you'll be absent again.

And this crippling fear makes me hold on to anything;
To pain, to terror itself and the dreadful imagery that the mind creates.
My body's uprising seems less scary than reality and so I allow myself to believe it architects plans against me.
I hold on to it.
To fear.

This frightened dog that barks at the void.
This withering but lasting light.
This is who I am without you.

LONGING

Where have we been, you and I?
The post office has been closed for months
There are dusty footsteps on the sidewalk and
Only the skeletons of the leaves catch the concrete floor.

I feel as if I was born inside this waiting,
And it never decreases,
The clock never turns the right way,
There's an absence that never goes away.

I grew with a longing no one ever learned to embrace
Nor understood how to fulfil
Without taking pieces out of me,
Because they never really fit in myself,
And I can't push them further.

Suddenly, I can feel the weight of waiting for you,
I perceive the white hair that grows out of me
I touch things on the verge of becoming dust,
And I spit my anxiety and my impatience into poetry.

It is late…

Outside the window, a dark night crawls over the sky
A black widow ready to kill lovers at first sight.
And those who long too much,
Caught on suspension,
Leaning on the windowsill,
Searching for that same old thing they cannot name,
The ghosts over our shoulders and what we cannot
pronounce.

The end of each verse is the end of the line.

I wipe the mask off my face before the mirror that judges
me.
The weary mirror with whom I've been sharing this wait
Since we first learned how to gaze
Into each other's eyes.

Sometimes I just stop at the sound of my voice,
As it remembers your own, and the sounds
A fork makes as it drops to the ground,
The way a sheet of paper rubs one's skin.

Maybe the sound of his voice at the back of my mind,
Similar to my neighbour's, makes me stop.
For mere seconds it all comes back
And I can almost taste the end of the waiting,
Then something vulgar and urgent catches my attention,
And the clock wins over again,
Filling me with the longing I have been digesting
As far back as I can remember.

POURED PROMISES

I'll take this forward; this promise of yours.
I have it stamped on my warm cheeks, salt streams separate
The lonely from the loved and remembered.

Maybe you forgot me, but I still carry it.

I thought I was engulfed in a hurricane, surrounded by the
violent wind,
Displaying more force than I could breathe with, distorting
my words.
I saw myself
As the Queen of Ephemeralities.
I was breathless, yes, because I've been swallowing waves of
thunderous air.
Aside, a whole sea is pouring from and into me.

Your words, then, were lifesavers. Full of will to lift me.
They were lighthouses and I held on to them, the careless
commitments.
I vowed to be their rescuer, feet strong against the current.
I'd shut my mouth and eyes; I'd be all ears to you.
You'd guide me to the sacred lands.

Your verses are the boat I board to escape the blood-clot
depths of my thoughts.
I've been hanging on to them until I'm strong enough and
you expel me,
Blood and guts and tears into the new world.
I cry loudly. The bright lights are terrifying. There's nothing
to hold;
Many hands constraining and pushing me away from you.

I found you in hidden paragraphs and vocalized your
promise.

The one I take with me, the one that delivers me back to the sea.
This is not the place to be, but here lies my peace.
Salt pours from my eyes, from my breasts, and down my legs.
You're a siren.
I hear you dive deep into the ocean and search, but never find my hollow shell
But the more I listen, the more I give in.
My arms and legs stop trying; the fight is too heavy

Droplets of ocean water kiss my lips and I cease to breathe completely.

I become another ounce in the pool of humanity, overflown.
I'm the reservoir behind the eyes of a new girl that mourns
A promise she does not remember.

INVITATION

Today is one of those proper days
For you to make a gaudy entrance,
For you to wake as if someone was knocking at the door
Half-asleep and half-angry, softly complaining.

You'd open up like a dormant flower, hands wet with dew
drops.
I'd crawl in and invade the warmth of your robe
The synthetic sigh of the heater would answer me,
You would create a whole melody for it.

Today there's still enough time for you,
For the stains of black lead on the couch
As you rotate the sketchbook to make a faithful
Portrait of the curves of my eye lines.

There is an empty space you could fulfil
Under my dome,
reliable for one night.
Not as supportive,
Much more precarious.

Today I could use a solid harbour,
As you were never able to be.

I could hand you this perfect opportunity
To embellish this day *by just being*
By just fully existing
Around me and under me and over me,

And amidst me as spilt glass,
As a malfunctioning shower,
As the rain that never bails on wetting the floor.

You could wash me all over,
With a gentle rush of water,
Sweet as only love's tears can be.

This is the long awaited chance
To transfuse your history into mine
To make the strenuous walk alongside
As if nothing, not even a single year,
Was concluded before.

Today, the stones and the flowers could be patterns,
On that old blanket in which you rocked me to sleep,
You could break the silence of your typewriter
To leave a note on the counter:
"Be home by noon. Wait for me."

It wouldn't matter if it's true,
I'd believe in you because, if there's something I'm good at,
It's in believing that the world would never turn towards
A time without you.

COMPOSITION

I am not this thought of you.

I see how you stare in awe and wonder,
Searching for an explanation,
Trying to understand how things connect,
Conjecturing who I am and how I got here.

Imagining which parts are really mine,
Which were given and which were stolen.
Wondering if I'd break to pieces or if I'm well fixed,
Under the right pressure.
You ask me if my words are my veins or my tendons
Do they flow through me or do they move me?
You really want to know.
You want my actions to be predictable and easy,
But I'm an earthquake, convulsing,
Exhorting stones against you.
Not even the grass below me is stable
And I wouldn't walk over me if I were you.

EVOKE

Evoke me
Recite poetry aloud, this tongue of dead languages, severed.
I am what got lost between words, the breath stuck inside the
throat.
These lines are my last trail of blood,
And my face is a frame where worn-out quotes come to die.

Evoke me with the vibrations of phonemes
So that I could be reborn into the world with renewed hope
Taking verses in and out to play,
Passing through life avoiding the dismay of having enough
thoughts
But not enough inspiration to make an impression.

Evoke them,
The ones that came before me, the ones who walked this
earth
Before I learned the syllables and the sounds.
Call them in, their fears and their freedom amounting on the
table
As brand new sheets of paper
Waiting for the caress of a poem.

Evoke those
Who make sounds in my ear as I try to fall asleep.
The siren that sings in a solemn tone, luring my courage
down
To the bottom of the ocean.
The hermit that forgot how to speak, but murmurs an entire
plot
Before her cigarette turns to ashes in her mouth.
The magician who enchants ravens and melts their black
feathers to ink.

Evoke the sounds of poetry,
The last shovel of dirt over someone's eyes, the sharp scissors
that separate
A child from its mother and welcomes new life.
The lament and the laughter, intertwined, that reside inside a
poem.

HAUNT ME

I woke up from another world.

There you were, in a green and white stitched dress,
Matching the curtains and the oppressive furniture, balanced
like a painting.
Nobody realized you chose the darkest place, behind the
windows,
Where the sun could not reflect how you really felt.

Both of us inside separate jars, segregated by frail walls of
glass,
Soundproof, waiting for us to dare a bolder move but we'd
never
Have the guts to break the divide, while the crowd expects
our composure to
Ensure us a title of adequate writers, women, humans.

I called you, as I always do in my mind, as I rarely do out
loud.
I called you three times. I rested my hands on your knees as I
plead:

"Please, look at me."

Your brown hair waved, easily moved by the few currents of
wind trespassing the windows and the open doors.
What an oppressive room!
Why are we here?

You didn't listen to me, you could not.

Maybe the touch wasn't even your skin against mine but a
sort of veil,
This shroud that divides our chances between dead and alive.

This dream was already dead.

I thought I could linger a little bit more. Turn this visit into
my own fantasy.
Then I thought I could wake up and discover we've
disconnected, nothing ever happened, nothing ever existed.
I'd be someone else.
Or it would be some other time. Some different world.
The view would be another, the landscape not made of
buildings.
I would not be made of my body; you'd still be made of
yours.

*Maybe I'd wake, hear your name for the first time and it wouldn't mean
a thing.*

Maybe I wouldn't carry this angst of losing my chance to
make you see me.

Because this longing will never go away.

There is no place where we'd eventually meet and go out for
a drink, for a laugh, for a chat.
There is no distant island, no mansion, no shack, nowhere I
could venture
A possibility of us being a family again. Or friends. Or any
existing link.

We're haunting each other for a chance of being listened.

We're the voices that raise us from our sleep, the distant calling we never
Fully recognize, and that terrifies us because, somehow, we want to follow.
We're the uncomfortable feeling of being constantly accompanied that
Should scare, but only teases us to unravel this that has been hiding before
Our very eyes.

We open them wide.
We want to see.
We want to answer.

Answer me.
Haunt me.

THAT KIND OF DAY

Blank days.

Like the wallpaper you poke carelessly,
So I wear and assume a flamboyant mask.
But some days are dull and cold as the walls beneath it.

Those are the days that go unnoticed.
You know them from the start.
The clock turns and no one realizes.
Eventually, you see it's 2 a.m.
And you can't remember what brought you to the moment.
You cannot recall what was done of the past hours.
The day just swoops you with its drabness.

Anything you eat on a day like this is bland, insipid,
You never feel satisfied but you also do not feel hungry.

You eat by habit. You drink by habit. You breathe by habit.

You shower because your apathy is blatant. Maybe water will
do it.
Maybe sleep will do it.

It doesn't. Not even your words seem to come together.
Either they are too aloof or over dramatic, and you don't
know
Where you fall on the spectrum. Perhaps right in the middle,
Hard to catch. That colour impossible to paint, that high
note,
That word that dictionaries miss.

The nights are worst.

Familiarity distancing, silence,
Everything seems completely out of reach and lethargic.
Reason falls into a coil, clogged. *What a mess to bring it back up.*
Your eyes are heavy and vision takes its time to become
cognition.
Counting minutes to midnight as if the mind works on shifts.

Who's to say what a bad day is?

THE PLOUGH

Some days don't ever fully bloom.

They dawn as smalls seeds, drooling with potential
The shy sprout forces through the floor.

But then something pulls it back,
Maybe a hungry weed, maybe aridness,
Maybe even an overflow,
And it refrains its ideas and dreams as if they were wrong.

It agonizes for hours,
The contractions of lost labours.

Until it diminishes, exhausted and eager
For the plough of the night.

GREY SKIES

The grey skies do not bow to anyone,
Not even me, the blurred figure walking
Wrapped in drastic measures and anxious resolutions.

I wish I could make something out of this feeling.

If I had hands for pottery, if my fingers were stable enough,
I could break vases against the wall,
I could give a name to my emptiness and gorge it out
Into a canopic jar, like Egyptians would pour organs
For a sanctified afterlife.

But I cannot.

My craft is to simmer the same feelings, an overcooked fear,
And I just season it a different way, I just make it taste
Better or sweeter.
Mostly it remains as bitter as it has always been,
Brewing inside me; same precarious fear.

I want to cure the pain of my beloved.

I want to suture wounds, I want to be good enough.
A strong form of miracle, touchable to be believable,
And yet surrounded by mysticism,
Because perhaps I don't want to be entirely human.

I want the grey skies to bow to me, not in fear,
Not in respect,
But in communion. In harmony.

It is impossible to be human and harmonious.

Even our innermost cells are designed in chaos,
Even our blood currents crash against each other.

The flow pulls me inwards, the ebb wastes me,
But either way, I'm always leaking through some
unperceivable hole.

If only I knew how to make more with this water,
I'd swim miles, I'd cross oceans, I'd save baby turtles that
amount
Over my bare feet.

But my craft is not the ocean.

It is the wall of seaweed that captures
Unaware fish and plastic cutouts from bottles and other
garbage
People leave behind.

I gather it all.

I'm always holding onto things that have no purpose,
While the blue whale weaves its tail,
And opalescent shoals swim by me.

If I could paint their tones, the metallic scales shining,
Perhaps the world could be fantastic,
And this old skin I hold on to could shed, showing
Wings I didn't know I had.

The grey skies never imagined I was bothered by them.

They imagined I was crying to keep water in synchrony,
To respect the tide, to comply with the moon.
They also did not foresee I was able to fly,
Because, well, neither did I.

I want to get soar so high the grey mantle would stick on me.

And with my absence, I could allow the sun to shine
Over everyone else.

I could take the grief away.
But the grey skies do not bow, not even for me.
So I may just as well remain.

CONDENSATION

The profusion.
Your many cells dividing and multiplying.
The sultry air in the greenhouse,
The moist earth I fertilized.
Suddenly, it's springtime and you're everywhere.

You're framed by the windows
Defying air on the second floor.
You're a whole library fecundated by ifs and whys.
My myopic eyes sculpt the shadows
The compound, the folding table, the wet towel.
They gather to resemble you.

An insurmountable jury and their laws.
It's acceptable to become bits of you, they convict.
Fingers behind the curtain,
Lips biting ripe figs, sweet drips on the floor,
The strand of hair and the thread of your dress;
I find blue fibres and yellow filaments everywhere.
The bone marrow rises from the dirt,
Roots crackle the vase searching for more and more space.
You're a jungle full of wildlife and poison.
The angry bees dancing, drinking and buzzing,
I'm afraid they'll plunge their gluttonous knives into me.
Don't run. They like to kill slowly...

I'm on the green nosocomial corridor.
My swollen limbs tied down by their own size.
You stare at me, at my numbness, at the blank napkins

You're the egotistical antidote I never refuse to take in.
I go back to sleep a motionless trance,

You're a sentinel by the dehydrated door,
Collecting my arid blood, sweat and tears,
Pouring yourself as torrid rain above me.

DON'T LET ME BE A TEAR

Gutted, I pull myself on a leash to a new day,
Along with many women, bleeding, tearing down their spirits
as old clothes.
Everything that bonds us is blood. From our legs to our
heads,
Our broken noses, our torn out vests, our emptied wombs.
Yet we leave our houses not knowing how much blood will
remain.

I'm completely exhausted sitting on the edge of my bed and I
don't know why.
Blaming my body, my mind, my organs. I want them to give
me reasons.
My energy feels like a dense liquid, spread on the floor and I
have no strength
To curl my spine and pick it back up. My skin is paper thin,
repeatedly punched
And the holes let my belongings escape; I guess they were
never mine
In the first place.

My neighbour cries. I cry too, but on alternate days.
Through windows that never stare at each other, we
share the pain
Of being women.

I am about to cross the street and a bus full of lights, teeming
with life,
Competes with the mourning that rises from the concrete.
There's a name on the sidewalk and I don't want to step on it,

I don't want to erase the pain because it is the only remnant of loss.
We cultivate it like the grass that dares to grow between the cracks.

Today I passed through four cemeteries. The gravestones did not look at me.
The angels turned their backs on the living. Our wounds far from heavenly.
We give flowers to the dead because they wither quick as our memories.
Our biggest fallacy is that we forget. Our biggest relief is that we forget.

If I am meant to be ephemeral, I want to be water.
I don't want to be a quick draught of air from a mouth saying my name.
I don't want to be the dancing candle flame that precedes the darkness.
I don't want to be a handful of ashes flying until they disappear.
If I have to be quick, I wish to be a stream. A healing gulp of water.
I want to revolve around a new life being formed.
Run to the sea with all my brief existence mixed with eternity.
I want to be rain over the driest regions.
I want to be the salty sweat of a protest.
Let me swim to where they went before me.
But, please, don't let me be a tear.

I'M BAD WEATHER

Eating dark skies. Heavy heart.
I push rains inside and down,
Way down until they cannot pour.
My body feels like a dark cloud about to wash away
everything in between
The ground and myself.
My head, a tempest. *I might give birth to hurricanes.*

Secretly, I hope they'll lift me high enough to run away.
Chaos and fear made me dauntless.
If bricks fly towards every window, I honestly couldn't care
less.

I'm heavy and indulgent, swallowing anxiety by gallons.

My throat is black as a chimney, like lungs filled with nicotine,
Except my darkness comes from within. From a wave of
terror,
From the fears of the outside that collapse with my
unsustainable inside.
I can hear the cracks of it while trying to sleep. Fading voices
erupting
From the breaches of my bones, plaster moulds breaking to
nothing.

I won't dare to look outside. I don't want to face the place
I've always been.

My nails are torn and still, there's no tunnel on my wall,
no escape.

And I feel like a lie, a presage of bad weather.
A natural disaster waiting to happen. Maybe a needed one, to end life,
To end death. *To end every sort of misguided vibration.*

I might decide to erupt from every pore and clean the earth,
Give my love as a martyr romance.

I might become a piece of art in a museum, the grey shape of a woman,
And people will create their own stories about me and about the things I've seen.
They'll give me names. Lovers. An interesting way to die.
They'll entitle me to the pages of a book, someday.

And I won't have to say anything, just rain.

FROSTBITE

My back hurts.

A knock of cold water went over my head,
My arms, my knees.
The soft spots weakened, terribly open as wounds,
Forced to coagulate without bandages, without the warm flux
Of recovery.
A glacial era unfolds at the tip of my tongue, the snowballs at
my feet.

I'm not allowed to mention the gentle grasp of summer.

The Sun claims me as his mistress, but I've been taken,
Tightened and tauten by the ice cold shower.

My purplish lips and fingers seem ready to slip
But I refrain them, as bad as my lungs refrain the wind.
My steps benumb the soil, the bees fall asleep on my hands
And I'm tempted to sting myself, *to feel myself again.*

I desire the flaming prickle, the tingling veins rushing to
spread
Hot blood all over my body.

I want to scald myself.

A soup of my sacrality ready to feed the meek, the trembling
Mouths under the wintering cloak of hunger.
I break the walls of skin that compress me.
They do not melt but crack, loud,

A baby that finds no lap to drool on, no matter how much it cries.
Teardrops freeze before they hit the ground.

Salty stalagmites, acute points to pinch the adventurous, to impale the brave.
They surround me.
They attend to me as a mournful bride. I cannot run.
I must smile and carry this weight as the finest silk.

And the clock is ticking.
The only one unscathed by the sharp knife of ice.
Annoyingly turning and generating heat, but never burning.

All the aged ladies with aching bones, aching backs, aching thighs;
Winter is not gentle with his former wives.

THE LAST ONE STANDING

How many lives have passed by me,
And how many people have I been
That I cannot find peace in my own skin?

That these eyes and hands are not enough,
For me to understand how to remain put together?
How many faces had I in the past
That being singular seems so insufficient?

There's always something missing,
Something misplaced.

The wooden structures have been eaten,
But the dust still calls to me and I remember everything,
Not with the mind but with every shiver down the spine.
With every hole that opens up in my heart;
Letting escape the sounds of past lives.

The multiple voices I once had,
Scream together for me to remember
Or to return
Or to let go of them
Or to run-
But I'm blank and dull,
Holding strong,
As an infant holding the fingers of strangers,
Just because I want
To have my hands around something real,
Or as close to it as possible.

I have no veins nor arteries,
But pathways.

The memories find their way back to me
Without meaning, only imagery,
And this persistent lack of being.
Somehow, I'm fixated with this idea of myself,
Of a very old version of me.
So old it probably never existed and
Therefore, it's perfect. Always better
Than this new edition, unabridged yet unexplained.

Perhaps,
So explained that it has become boring.

An instruction book instead of poetry.

I'm brand new yet so full of dust,
So full of footnotes and asterisks
Because I want to make sense.

I want to be this important part of history,
This archaeological find,
The Queen of the Nile in hardcover.

But maybe, I am only the paperback,
The feeble page marker,
Of my past, more important selves.

UNSUSTAINABLE

It's trying to escape, you know.
My spine
Right through my head.
I can feel the poking,
The calcium needle, protruding.

But it has nowhere to go, you say,
And then the sound.
The sound.
The sound.

People don't understand
The concept of silence.

I try to teach them through example,
Because my spine is ratcheting
And the vibrations of my voice
Could make it leave faster.

It is not a threat, though.

It is not a menace
Or a vengeance.
It is not an eviction notice,
Or a broken relationship.

It's just,
I've become,
Un
sus
tain
a
ble.

I am not trying to keep it inside,
I respect the privacy of my spine,
Doing its own thing,
But I'm trying to suture it in a way
That every piece will remain in place.

I'm stitching heart onto lungs
Onto fat onto liver onto stomach
Onto legs onto bladder
Onto muscles
Onto gristle.

People don't understand the concept of silence
Or, I don't understand the concept of language.

Maybe if I say
hey,
My spine is leaving…
But it doesn't like to call attention to itself
And neither do I.

There's no need to explain
Why I've been folding onto myself;
It is a good thing,

LONGING

Not being still.

This spine is not mine
Not anymore,
It's not a flag plunged to declare property.

We were here of common accord,
And knew one would have to leave
Eventually,
To find new things to bear,
To hold in place.

My spine needs more solidification,
To be calcified,
And I need more flowering
To be satisfied.

Flexible as a stem
That might grow mold
And liquify,
But is not afraid of blossoming,
As my spine has always been.

YOU BAILED ON ME

It could have been an August morning just like this.
Probably colder, with a blanket over the sky, but similar
enough.

The Sun was there, the same old Sun.
The true witness of our mistakes.

He was quiet behind the clouds as a tired father that,
After lecturing his children about how viscid mud can be,
Simply cleans the floor and throws their tiny boots in the
trash.

The disobedient children wait for the quarrel but it never
comes,
Just a gloomy silence penetrating the halls.

On a morning just like that, with the Sun exhausted of trying,
You bailed on me.

I could hear the crackling of our crumbling trust.

There was so much pain between us.
Each shard of glass pervading our palms was a lost chance.
Your bad thumb, with the black nail pointing out,
Could crumble completely by this disruption.

You bailed on me.

The guts you've promised to have,
The guts you've strangled me with,

They were not enough and so weren't we.

Time was wrong.

History made a huge mistake.

The Sun remained silent and I don't know if out of love or
cowardice.
The Moon would have said something.

She would have screamed out her rays,
She would have made the flow between us so outraged by
this rupture,
They'd make us nauseate at the glimpse of this mitosis.

But you chose to leave me during the day.

You chose to write me out beneath the sun,
After two nights of sleeping with your eyes open.
After resting in front of the heater,
Blaming the weather for your shaking hands.
When the day finally began and the dew smelled of hope,
You bailed on me.

EMANCIPATION

My first memory of you was tearful.
I could not name it yet, I wasn't supposed to know
What sorrow meant but I could recognize you
Inside my cries.
You were the muffled things I wanted to say,
But they pacified and silenced me, because I shouldn't
Understand pain as heavy as this.

Emptiness was the real title of my core.

I'd echo anything.
A black canvas waiting for a dose of light, for a white streak
of paint.
The reverse expectations waiting for what I have never seen,
But could describe perfectly. You pervaded the room
As a freshly cooked tray of biscuits. Sweet, good, and
soothing.

I felt hungry for you, a primal hunger.
I swallowed draughts of air.
I swallowed the sound of old poetry.
You were inside the voids, above and beneath my hands.
I became so tired of praying to recognize the tone of your
voice.

I listened to nature.
Every Mockingjay wanted to tell me something.
The wind passed screaming through my ears.
Suddenly the world was angry at my lack of understanding.
I felt useless.

Your frustration took the form of a dying trail of bees.
I'd rescue them by the dozen to try to rescue me.
Honey became insipid, I felt I could not enjoy the sweetness
of life,
Unless you'd enjoy it with me.
But you were not here. Nor will you ever be.

Time can turn haunting into reliability.

True emptiness is feeling you're not here and I'm all alone,
With the ferine words that want to dismember me alive.
And I don't mind the pain but I must be holding your hands,
To guide me through the dark pit after I fall.
After we both fall, pushed by a good poem.

The more you are around, the more you seem to be vanishing
As a learned lesson.
To walk I must leave the ground but you've made laying
down so comfortable.

I don't think I'll ever want to go.

Just the same as I need you, you need me. To keep the
candles lit,
To keep company as we lay mutually on the portal before it
closes.
We make promises impossible to fulfil just for the sake of it.
I want you to be proud, you look as if you already were.

We both know it is not true.

To make you proud I must leave.

I must live in the right time zone.
Bid farewell to the sole certainty of my life.
To the first memory of a tear, so filled with sorrow,
I even learned how to smile just to sustain it.

But every time I open the door, I must look back
To find your arms wide open. To find stillness.
I must accept that being born is dying somewhere else.
I'm finally here. And, in my living sadness, I'm free.

BEES DIE PEACEFULLY

Of course, the sun was out today.
Luminous and infuriated as you liked it, throwing up rays,
Making my skin boil into a vermillion I've never seen before
And my eyes glitch, somehow making me believe you were
The faces I crossed on the streets.

The sun's homage made the concrete leak and my certainties
dissolve,
Paving roads I never considered walking on but now they
seem
So secure and so easy to believe in that I might just go,
Pack my ragged bags and roam.

Questioning is tiresome when you don't receive an answered comfort.

The crude moment when you must admit that your observant
bench does not have answers,
You have to seek the truth out, even though they want you to
believe you're not ready to hear it.
Some eyes are good at convincing you of incapacities.
You may find them around, you may find them at home,
You may find them on the other side of the mirror.

The concrete beneath the sun felt like quicksand.
Your feet stuck into warm white sand at the beach and you,
running around,
Ankle-deep cold water vamping you into the sea, each time
more,
And I could do nothing but watch, complaining about the
things we'd miss

If we left late, not knowing how much I'd miss by leaving
early.

Eventually, you gather all the things you have and leave,
because you need
To find something with more syllables.
A complex explanation for this absence, rather than
coincidence.
Coincidence is choosing an outfit the same colour as the car
upholstery.
Coincidence is taking a new path, and ending up in a street
that's the
Name of a place you wanted to go

Coincidence is a moment. If it lasts for years, you need a new
designation.

I felt descending into the underworld, into Hades, as I took
the escalator,
Leaving behind the summer and entering a world of
unending cold.
Me and my short dress, as a childhood dream giving space to
real life.

Another reason why you loved the sun was that you knew it
would set.
You loved things that you could be assured to have an end.

If beauty lingered for longer, you'd proclaim it not beautiful
anymore.
The day was only valorous because it rescued you from the
night.

You only loved the moon because you could tell when it
would appear
And for how long it would stay hidden.
And you only cared for me because you knew how to keep
me, and how to let go of me,
With a single push, a forced labour to restrain love
From growing inside your loins for more than acceptable.

You only kept the things you could control.

There are tarot cards spread in front of me.
I can hear the scratch they leave on the table as they turn to
be revealed and the answer is not there.
Nor was it on the leaves of my tea or my jaundicious hands.
I had to recognize that nothing would tell me words unsaid.
The answers are not word wise; they are the hushes I hear at
night.
They are the sight of your typewriter across a pristine glass,
The shift in the wind when your name is spoken out loud.

A wasp landed on my windowsill to die.
It does not move and does not try to fight against my
presence.
In the last moments, I guess we lose our fears.
You said that bees died peacefully because they knew their
work was done.
That once the burden of leaving something behind was lifted,
they'd collapse in absolute bliss, a triumphant trail of black
and yellow stripes.

I felt like you'd leave just the same, as soon as you had
something to be proud of.

As soon as you felt that you were repeating the same words
and no new verbiage could fulfil you; you would open your
wings and fall straight to the floor.
Honey dries, honey ends.
But not yours, and you knew it.
The answer is sweet, but the source is out of reach,
And I am more the resigned wasp than the accomplished bee.

But of course, the sun was out today, just the way you liked it.
The beekeeper's touch never leaves the hive.

EMBERS

Whatever it is that wanders from me to you, this shadow that
has no name,
This feeling almost impossible to catch but embroidered onto
our skins,
This towering love and craving, no language bothered to
explain,
Because it never existed before and maybe never ever will
exist again.

So I take upon myself the journey of making it substantial.

This is the fuel that puts my hands on a burning spree,
That precludes me from lifting from my seat until I've put it
all out.
Until I'm completely drained, open without modesty, without
shame.
Not unless I've thrown myself beyond the embers, each with
a scorching limit,
Each trying to make me give up and telling me that, if it was
meant to be, then
I wouldn't burn.

But it's my skin's ability to reconstruct, to reclaim its right to
be whole again,
That makes this the right path.
The scars we carry are a dictionary for this uniqueness.
Burning is another way of writing and healing is a page-
turning way to love.

Let's incinerate a whole novel together.

POETICAL ANTHROPOPHAGY

I go from one obsession to another,
From one past to the other as if it could save me.
My arms hurt from begging to deaf walls to hear me,
Pushing it all back into life, fitting meat into skin
Breathing into the lungs of history.

I attach myself to things that feel safe,
Doesn't matter how deeply they cut,
They are unchangeable and, therefore, they must remain
By my side, after it all fades.

I paint the eyes of my obsessions, from green to grey,
In such vivid tones, they have no other choice than stay,
And look at me from the other side of the bed.
One caresses my head as the other caresses my skin,
And I'm protected from the omnipresent reality.

I can dive undercovers when they arise from fate.

They have such beautiful names I fill the air with.
Every shade of auburn hair amuses me,
As a reminder they're around as a never-setting day,
And I ricochet from here to there easily,
Pages turning back and forth from the same old book.

This is how I've learnt to make love.
Through words and pages and the lustful way an avid reader
devours each sentence to digest a full poem.
The way one must wet your lips to make it sound properly.

The same way we've been reading each other,
Anthropophagically.

LINOLEUM

It's been raining all day.
I'm shedding pieces onto the white floor.
The borders are flowing with hair and dust and short strings
of web.
I'm an extravagant cloud,
A cumulonimbus, sleepwalking,
Moving with the silence of broken glass.
My cat can't play outside because my tempest blocked out the
doors.
We're locked inside, avoiding the floating furniture.

I attempt to stop the rain and the flow and the ebb
But it does not,
It would not,
Not until I'm all afloat.
The deck of my skin is empty,
Soaking wet,
Not even a single step to testify
The rain and the vastitude of this ocean
I became.

The water is clear and it shines underneath
I see my stretched feet,
I'm a bridge
Between the land and the skies.
The sun is out now,
Sparkling in the linoleum tiles,
Clamours of stainless land.

LOST DAYS OF SUMMER

I never knew your youth.
The light smile and the carefree glance.
The way you'd hold tight to a drinking glass,
Your red nails like snakes undoing your boredom,
Teasing the hopeful boys gathered by your door,
Just for the sake of having something to write about.

I believe our lives crossed later on,
When your smile was unsustainable by itself.
No. It needed a lift.
An exact sun ray in an exact piece of skin,
A new word from your baby girl's lips,
A brand new cake recipe and a firm frosting,
A tall glass of brandy to entwine your fingers around.

There were no more boys at the porch, no more lines,
But a man at the door.
Sometimes, he'd stay as far as the gate,
Sometimes, he'd climb up the stairs into your bedroom,
He'd lift a box or two as a favour and you'd think
Three times before making the decision
Of keeping cold and sturdy as a rock.
Inside you, a flower was dismantled
Only the thorns piercing through the skin.
He'd blame you for the pain he'd inflict.

When we met, you were young,
But your sadness was old and grey as a weary cat,
Stray and hungry for something the streets could not give,
Tired of so many lives and losses.

You had a weight on your shoulders that I could feel
Just by being around you, even though,
You'd still wear your best smiles for me.

Those you kept locked for important days,
You had a handful of those.

I remember when you wore the last one.

I remember how you stared at your old pictures,
Trying to recreate the teeth, the lips,
The pressure on your cheeks and your chin.
You faced the mirror for two hours that day
Knowing something was lost forever,
You could not replace that last smile.
How hard it was for you to sleep that night,
Aware that it would fade.

You had the worst nightmares.

When you woke up even the sky was mourning.
There was no exact sunray to bathe in,
All the cake recipes were outdated and musty,
The sink had a pile of dishes with all the things you could not
eat,
Your mouth was an insipid piece of paper
Contoured with a strong lipstick.
From the hole, only water would flow in
And then out again with digestive juices and angst.
You ran out of nursery rhymes.
You ran out of promises.

You ran out like a dry faucet,
Turning loosely on your axis,
Hoping to be dizzy enough to fall asleep.

I never knew your days of summer
And maybe that's why,
Resentfully,
The season's warmth bothers me.

INFLAMED MOTHS

I followed the old beacon again,
A mirrored moth attracted to darkness.
I let it suck on me,
I let its suckers adhere to my skin.

My wings are inflamed,
Swollen,
And when they beat, they hit each other,
So it is too painful to fly
But it's too painful to stand still
Because the darkness can also burn,
And it's burning.

My wings have a fever and there's no medicine,
No treatment to soothe the heat,
Only the violent flap
That hurts and tears them to pieces.

PRESCRIPTION

I need you today because things are oddly unfitting.
I am a spawn, chewed up and spat in the fat hands
Of a spoiled child that doesn't care about things that disappear
forever under the bed.

I need your presence because everything seems terribly cold
Under this summer sun. There's glass over us and everything
inside is freezing.
My blood seems to run thick as a snow mass on a tight
corridor,
When I move, sharp shards of ice stick out from my bones.
One more step and I might crack entirely, joining the rest of
those
That stood inside this barren glass structure before.

I need you because I don't know what to say anymore.
I don't know what to claim my own, how to stand tall on a
ground that never stops turning.
You'd look at me and apologize, explaining that you cannot
be a guide.
That you have no idea where you're stepping and that you
lost your foot
And your good thumb trying to figure it out.
But it does not matter. I want to cling on to the journey, to
the company,
Even if we have absolutely no idea what's ahead of us.

I need you to reflect me properly through your eyes, because
the mirror stopped cooperating and it refuses to swallow my
existence.

I do not know who's looking back, who got sorted out to
replace me,
And I don't think we'll become acquaintances in such a short
time.
Your clear hazel pupils knew what to contain,
And what to let go, to create the world in an orderly way,
And how each atom should be positioned and constructed
over another.

I need you even though I know you won't understand what I
mean.
You never had the chance to hear my cries and to decipher
my language,
So you might mistake my solitude for hunger or contentment.

You could step into the kitchen and wonder, hands running
through the hair and back to the waist, if you're missing
something.
In the back of your right lobule, there's a hidden song and a
meaning.
But whenever you're close to grasping it, it vanishes, because
the neighbour
Dropped something on the floor or the cars buzzing muzzle
the sound at the front door.

I need you in exact portions to fit my mouth, to embrace me,
to give cover
To my weakness and dress my powerful traits.

You'd never cry like Pietà because your sorrows had a unique
translation,

Your lap was a merry-go-round, not a motionless nest.
I remember spinning around, not developing wings but a strong hoof,
So I could step on broken glass without risking my tendons.

You taught me that the bad wolves are safer than the woodsmen.
I'd never commit your mistakes and that was our agreement.

I need you standing on the other side of the harbour of my eyes.
Encouraging me to swim harder because you've missed me and need a hug,
And I'd give my best against the current, legs and feet punching the water
In search of shelter and rest. *I cannot struggle anymore.*

All I see is the unchangeable dark blue glow and I thought I heard you,
In the wind, in the waves, in ephemeral things I cannot keep
I cannot look twice and if I blink, away you go again.

I need you to tell me that the monsters will disappear if we don't answer the door,
That the bad things get just as tired as we do and it's all a matter of waiting,
Until one side drops the rope and withdraws.
You had such a strong conviction, it resonated through the walls of your skin,
And turned fear into a war cry without a word.
I was invincible then.

I need you as dying things need to go back to their source.

As a wounded animal goes back into the cave of its cubhood,
In search of a figure that will never be there except for tufts
of fur.

I enter the place from which I was so prematurely disposed,
In search of a crutch to lean on because the outside took the
best of me,
**And I need to isolate myself from the outer world before
I'm all gone.**

That's what I need you for.

SPLINTERED

Like a splinter in my finger you are.
The acute remain of something beautiful.
The more I try to remove you,
The deeper you sink and swell into my being.

Not even the blood trickles to decompress.
My interior seems to be ordering an army for a battle,
Yet we succumb to something so small
And unannounced as you.

I exchange syllables as dying men exchange wounds
For hope, for a chance of peeking through the windows,
And finding green meadows over stones.
But I aim higher than any dying man should.
I have a relentless desire for kissing the skies.
You demand a greater risk and a rarer disease,
You demand a ritual and a mending of hearts.
To heal this wounded finger, my body could collapse,
And still not be healed at all,
And still, sting at the root of my core,
Flushed by the patterns you represent
So avidly and so well spent.

A nice saleswoman you are
The fine print enrols me as a mahogany door
You'd open and close at will,
Transient and ephemeral, almost see through,
And I must be content stepped on, unlocked and
remembered
During the day,

As something you may have forgotten,
Such as the gas or the lights or the iron,
Such as the necklace pending on your bed.
You feel naked without it but overcome the absence.
You may even come back home with another,
Cheaper, easier and almost fulfilling.

The tweezers scuff my skin in search of you,
Buried deep as my worst sins.
Unknowingly, I've hammered the splinter down
Until you're every piece of furniture,
Every tree,
And every wound.

NOT ENOUGH

There is still so much…

I tiptoe to you as a toddler learning how to stand still,
Ricocheting between your arms and the coffee table.
At the top of my trembling feet, I think I know the world
I believe I've discovered everything and,
Most importantly,
I think I know you, completely.

I've been drowning inside your name and the many times I've
said it,
Again and again as a mantra, as a religion to which
I've converted from birth.

Baptized by the air that comes out
Of each mouth that ever said a word about you.

But there is still so much left unsaid that the drowning of
your name becomes a lake,
Ankle-deep high.
I'm not even wet.
The soaked up feeling evaporates,
The weight of my damp clothes is actually the weight
Of this endless search, this archaeological endeavour,
After your trails.

There is still so much…

I hear the doors slamming with an incommensurate violence.

Behind them, still as gargoyles, your secrets cry.
The hurt on your wrists and shoulders are soundless
But, oh my, they howl so high.

You've kept them silent as only written words can be.
I try to take the door down and it ignores me.
I breathe out the idea that you are on the other side,
The fear that, if I don't open it fast enough,
The hints will disappear and it will all be in vain.
My hands unravel the flock of keys I've gathered
With a childlike belief that I could figure you out,
And bring your secrets and masked tribulations to light.

There is still so much...

The baggage I've collected seems massive.

I thought that, after knowing you this much,
I'd be rooted and content and pacified.
Only to discover I've been playing with the shallow,
Flat lines that do not screw into this structure.
And the languid walls crack, bellowing the oddest cries:

There is still so much more!

YOUR NAME

I'm flustered by the reading of your name.

It's a lit cigarette, once said, once stated.

It will keep on burning its enclosure and its surroundings,
And even those at a distance will be intoxicated.

It may take time, it may take a lifetime,
But you will get into their systems.

And the saying of your name becomes no different
Than the explosions of Nagasaki and Hiroshima.
Then there's the waves, the continuance;
The blasting of your name does not end on the syllable.
It goes on, the bells toll progressively,
The echoes ricochet at the muscles and the gristles.

From the moment I first heard it,
I had to go back to learning
The language, the writing, the enunciation,
Never the same, always impaired by the stating of your name.

The letters slip from my mouth with my breath,
Almost forming in the air as a massive cloud of smoke,
But I inhale it back, the flux of your reputation,
Never parting, eternally refusing to let go.
I stand by the ashtray where you raise immaculate;
You and your rim blackened as the night
Do not respect my weary mind,
my tiredness.

And goes on and on,
Mouthing,
Writing,
Carving,
The rapture of your name.

PROPER

I don't think I'll ever be.
Have the dexterity to spread over the right places,
Make the exact connections and trim
What is no longer necessary.

To clear the baggage after a learnt lesson.

I think I'd be stuck with the crumbs and dead bugs,
Caught in the fabric, instead of the gold carefully panned.
Then I'd throw it all back together, a tangled ecosystem,
Never fully separating the bad from the good.

Even the accurate rhymes, I might never orchestrate.
Always listening to a different tone, making sense inside my
head,
But rarely to the mind of others.
No audience would get up and cheer
Because there's the righteous rhythm and there's mine,
Sharing some notes but the full-scale falls, flat as a stone.
I'd probably be the tone-deaf conductor, elegant as a bird,
Lost and confused as a moth knocking its head against the
hot lamp.

I'm terrified, I have no clue whose hands are on the switch,
But I'll keep banging into the light to see what gives up first,
The wings or the glass.

THE EGRESS

Why are you leaving?
I see the door half open,
Your perfume's a thin strip,
And an empty pack of cigarettes on the table.

I exorcised you so many times before,
I fed you my fears and my plans for escape,
Until the walls caved in and I opened my weak arms,
Overflown, drowned and peaceful as a new-born.

Now you threaten me with your suitcase,
Staring at me from the porch, waiting for something I cannot
name.
You long for words I never even learned.
I, a supplicant animal, craving, digging my paws into the
ground!

You turn around, then back, then turn the flocks of your hair
Unsure as an amateur.
You always were afraid and aloof.
The world under your feet but not close enough,
Not far enough.

There lies your prison for letting me out.

For the awareness of your lap and your smell and your
lullabies,
If you turn the lock, if you shut the door…
Stay. The whole kingdom is chanting your name.

Stay. I cannot withdraw anymore.
I want to crawl back
To your pure chaos,
And our chords, strong and inflexible.

You stand at the door, pale.
Don't let me bleed out, I beg you.
How could you let me go unnoticed,
Dripping onto newspapers and poems?

You come back in.
The door crashes behind you.
I hold on to you as a lost child,
A broken toy you just can't throw away.

FILTERED

Something got lost, dormant at your doorstep,
A trail of words I carried carefully to bestow unto you,
But immediately they turned into liquid and slid down
Before I could drink it. Before I could retain or store it.
Something was instantly absorbed by your abandoned garden.

I had no tears.
I thought I'd shed gallons, but they were in disbelief.
They evaporated as a pleasant dream at the dawn of a bad
day.
I was all blood, fever, and breathless. I was sore knees in
front of you.
I was the inability to leave. I was the fear of being alone.
My hands wanted to touch everything while a persisting sense of violation
Pervaded my actions. I was not pure enough, for you, nor
anyone.

And I left parts of me that I didn't feel falling out.
I left vital organs and essential patches of thought.
Whole verses escaped me, flowing back to the source.
The maelstrom gave space to calm waters. So calm that
nothing came out.
A comatose sense of purpose.
I've been running to you for so long, I didn't know the other
side of it.
We remained in a dense silence, the one that follows a fight
or a confession.
I've been trying to break it ever since.

At nights, I hear knocks on my door, I hear words on my

pillow.

I hear the soft crunches of a trail of crumbs leading me back
To where I belong.
My most organic movements push me sideways to the edge
of the sea,
To the seams of who I had to be and who I want to be,
The one that does not hide anymore because it has a place to
exist.
I need to return to get my words back from you.

But if you spill them out, I don't know if they'll whither or
sprout.
    And neither which will I.

TACITURN

Under my feet
The soil disappeared, vanished in protest,
Not willing to carry me.

For months, my steps had been hurtful.
Angry stones would invade my boots and torture
The soles with tiny daggers and psychological games.
I transmute into a snail, a small package stuck on my back,
Crawling in the air, doing the best I can not to leave
A trail, because the floor is infuriated and I dread quarrels.

Words were also a problem.

The spoken, loud, room-filling words.
They'd always cause incidents, break the expensive porcelain,
Shake the bureau to the edge and create sudden earthquakes.

No room would gladly echo them, constantly bouncing off
the walls
And facing a strenuous resistance.

I found that swallowing them was the best alternative.

My throat was swollen but, like everything else, it became
accustomed.
I grew familiar with silence, with the tender sonance of typing
And my tongue languished, attached to disuse.
I could unscrew it effortlessly.

Slowly, I lost contact with words and time, between the here and there,

Like a baby hare, unsure of what the world means, watching
it all through the glass filter of placenta and feeding off the
past.

I make no noise as I transport from one place to another,

Just taking with me the remembrance of what I used to say,

And the places I used to walk,

And the eyes I used to see,

Before it all became a conflict.

THE WELL

We gather at the well of our dissatisfactions,
The denials stare deeply and I feel your cold hands
Each word is a second without a heartbeat,
Your haughty head so well disguised.
I yell at the well and it shrieks back at me.

My voice ricocheting and slipping through the bricks,
A gooey caucus of multiple cries,
And the hungry emptiness of underachieving.

You look down and then back up and refuse
To look any further.

I'm entranced by the way my blood thickens and boils,
The nauseating weight of my self-doubts.

The road before us narrows and widens,
As a cat's eye trying to absorb the world,
Now it seems unbearably limited, precarious,
On the verge of shutting down as a dense forest.

The stones of the well form an unsettling grin,
So pleased to see me stepping back and back and back,
It wants to swallow me as a humid spit.

But I'd go down caustic and pungent as an unfaithful kiss.

I wonder if you're an echo too.

If you're the words I utter at the world, lingering,

Packed together enough to create a feeling,
But not enough for an arm, a sound or a breath.

The well is now a black hole,
Eating every grain of our galaxy.
Each question feeds it with darkness and depth
And the more I ask the more I hesitate.
Our universe is collapsing with my disbelief.

Somehow, I have not awakened from this last dream,
And the world is muttering we should not pretend
That our minds will go the way we intend them.

The well is every comma, every unfinished phrase,
The well is the seer of our worst days.
How they combine into time, how we commune our diseases,
How our hands still dare write into the dark.

The bricks scratched and handwritten
With all of our attempts to swim through the tide,
Every failed shot piled up for either one:
Drown or quench our thirst.

POETRY PROPHET

I clump the clues as little mounds of wet mud.
A magnanimous collection of footprints you've left behind
And I harvest each one, my hands dirty,
My fingernails blackening as the bruised earth invades the gap
Between the skin and the keratin.

It is a life-threatening deal to love someone I cannot catch a
grasp of.

The weight of not knowing falls over me as if, on a summer
night,
While I dampen the sheets with sweat, someone throws a
heavy coat on me,
And I learn to live inside the heat. *I learn to burn continuously.*

Absence burns.

It is the oxygen that feeds this fire.
What an irony that the void of your existence is oxygen.
I can breathe the lack of you in and out. It pinches my lungs.
I'm a butterfly on a board, still struggling against the stake.
But, truth be told, I know I won't fly anymore.
The hollow cocoon has an eviction notice glued to it, in bold
red letters,
Tied to a wooden plaster board, hanging crooked on my heart
chamber.

I sink into this vanished love because I've been taught to
have faith.

So I accept to stare at the rain and find something more
inside each drop.
I see vulgar occurrences as evidence of my responsibility
To collect and maintain and protect from the outer
shallowness.

I walked by a pile of hay that resembled the colour of your
hair;
seeing references where I shouldn't,
It was wet and sad, facing down, as yours was after a cold
shower,
Or on the last day at the beach, when the sun was not excited
anymore
And you curled back inside as a shy flower.

I've kept it all out of faith. Out of trusting more than I see.
Some days, I say your name out loud, all alone, as a prayer.
Or I repeat it, obsessively, as a mantra; 108 times.

I even close and open my eyes thinking you'd appear.

Because love is nothing more than a blind belief,
And I am the prophet.

EPILOGUE

Winter is about to leave.
The remaining cold is not even trying anymore,
Sunrays escape through the clouds,
Just like when winter left you.

Years do not matter, they never did.
The same days marked by the filling of my lungs
Are stained by the deflating of yours.
By the countdown to when
It all became unbearable.
There was a day, a particular day when you realized that
The wave, towering, was about to crash.

That day had the smell of burnt all over it.
A disaster in the kitchen was remarkable as a natural
catastrophe.
The black smoke was a suffocating volcano, taking over a
village.

Your body static but vulnerable, ash stacked together but
sensible to a heavy breath.
You'd be blown away if the children began to cry that very
instant.
Your hands burned.
The tray, not at all distressed, fell to the floor making sure to
advocate for its sound.
A poisonous piece of silver commanded by the world to turn
against you.

You could feel the process of moving your arms:

From sending the orders to your brain to contracting your
muscles,
The torrent of blood running to make it react,
The palms of your hands blistering in agony.

Suddenly, existing seemed such a strenuous task.

That was the day you felt the feelings give way
To something darker and harder to grasp.
Something you could not avoid
Because it would swirl around and vanish in thin air by the
sound of a word,
By a leaf rustling, by the babies blabbering, or just by a
change of rhythm in your heartbeat.
It was impossible to take it, to clean it, to remove it from
where it was clinging to you.

You just felt it sucking all the other emotions into a dark pit
and, at first,
It resembled healing.

It deceived you into limpidness.

A nihilistic baptism to prepare for a new substance.
Your body a fertile field crowned by your head like the sun,
golden,
A seductive gravitational force for words and thoughts.

The scarcer the feelings, the faster your hands seemed to
type.
Beginnings and endings have such equality.
Each paper that flew from your left to your right took a drop

of you,
Until there was none.
You could even drown in such absence.

So devoid that you went unscathed into wholeness.

SAIL

I need to drown the tide that tries to overflow.
My throat and my face,
An inundation.

All I have is a wet napkin,
So I take the boat, shove the pill down my throat to my
rescue,
Which does not stanch the leakage
But calms the sea.

I've been searching for you inside the turmoil,
How typical of me to anchor myself to
Something this fragile.

I use distance as a safety measure,
And time as a life vest,
So when reality hits me,
I cannot fall any further than this.

Whenever I open my eyes,
After a rest, a whole night or even a blink,
There's hope you'll be there,
Staring at me,
Reaching out to me,
Reading the lines on my face,
Pointing out a piece of land I could not see,
But my eyes are wide open and I'm drifting.

MOLTEN

Have you ever stood at the root of a volcano?
Tiny grains of mauve sand stuck between your toes,
Raging warmth each second higher, a degree per step,
Until it's impossible for you to keep standing and your
Body just wants to give in because it feels weaker and frail.

My heart resembles this imminent eruption, and I'm standing,
Although I feel the trembling and hear the rocks banging
against each other.

My bird-like thoughts are scared, flying in circles knowing
something's not
Quite right, but no idea what's wrong and where to run.

There are flocks beside my kidneys, two stray doves pecking
at my intestine and
A pitch-dark raven in my stomach, stealing my strength and
refusing to leave
Because I owe him a safe nest, and this is the best I could
ever give.

My plumbing's too narrow for such pressure so the leakage is
inevitable,
Coming out as words, as stumbling in obstacles that are not
there,
As forgetfulness because my line of thought escapes to give
space to my breathing, to the hardware repair needed and the
cleansing,
After the birds and wild animals punished me for failing to
stop

The collapse of my own nature.

All those precious things I've been treasuring are at risk,
Because not a single room of my being can shut the doors of
The outburst of my heart when it decides it needs release.
And, though I feel inflammable, I fear the only thing
remaining
Will be a gunpowder outline of a person,
Burnt to the ground, hands shut on a sprout,
Almost dried out but still alive; somehow, still eager to
flourish.

INCITING MOUNTAINS

The tasks are piling up as mountains I must climb, ice cold
and slippery.
My shoes have huge holes in them and I'll have to give up my
limbs
In order to reach the top, even though the obligations never
end.
The peak's always more and more dangerous, leaving me the
tiniest space.
I must walk with my bare bones, leaving the flesh behind me.

Complaints are received with pills and snow to throttle down,
the cold grip scraping the walls of my throat with ancient
drawings.
My autopsy would be a brand new anthropological exposition,
The register of a past civilization,
A nomad pack duelling solitude with sharp sticks and heavy
stones.

I've been staring at things until they dissolve, and the liquid
runs through my fingers,
Nothing makes them stick like the density of the things I've
lost.

Those I cannot keep inside my eyelids because they tear out
of me as victims,
And I dehydrate with the losses and my own lack of
capability to pour into me
The same warm viscosity I shed for everyone else.

I never learned how to drink myself into proportion.

Either I flow or I fermentate, hidden inside an embrace I
cannot understand.
It could be the deathly circulation of a snake.
I cannot breathe.

But I must climb the enormous mountains. It seems so easy,
There are many obnoxious flags waving at me, stabbed deep.

Mine should be up there too, but there's no cheering.
Only charging.

Dozens of pendulums dictating my rotation and all I want is
to keep straight.
All I want is to go higher.
And still each step seems to lead me closer to a death-trap,
but I must keep
Smiling and climbing, nodding along.

The mountains threaten me with a landslide.
I cannot scream.

I can only climb.

LATE NIGHT HAIRCUT

There are too many names for anguish and too many flavours
for it.
My taste buds are saturated with the waves of pronounces I
have
For this feeling and still cannot spit it out, cannot eject it
down the drain,
So I have to remove pieces out of me to pay this toll.

My hair falls as bales of hay, creating a soft bed but I still
cannot name its design.
More and more and more, they leave me as overfed children.
The labour pains are numb, the razor is quick and deep as an
epidural.
Three long breaths and there goes another tangled new-born.
The sink is now a bassinet.
Intricate laces try to distract me from the layer of dust sitting
on my tongue.
I cannot expel and I cannot swallow this distress.

There's so much of me I'm letting go to ignore the weight on
my shoulder,
On my body, on my mind.
On the mirror, every time I have the guts to stare.
I'm cutting off the braids hoping each string of red hair is
Ariadne's thread,
Leading me out of the labyrinth, but the walls are reflective
and I wonder
If I'm the one I've been running from.

I'm the worst hybrid monster I know.

My hair is just a different type of fur, clogging the water, and
my words rise back again.
They'll never go down. The weight will be replaced
Each time, no matter how many parts of me I throw out,
There will be an equivalent hurt, a wig of issues I must face.

But for one night, I might feel lighter. The bathroom is
flooded,
The vocabulary swirling like sharks in woe, their cries echo as
a threat.
They claim I'm still the same.

The eyes that look at me through the water corroborate but,
for the first time,
The water's running from everywhere yet my eyes are dry.

REPO

The ache and the painkillers share one common thread.
They circulate my body, pulling a nerve here, tickling a
tendon there,
To see if it moves. To see how I react.
They tease me, propelling me to move, wondering if I am at
all unwell.
I am an object of study to my own fears.

The cold truth of the metal table burns my skin.
I wake up with bruises I didn't remember, hijacked by
another sense of self, a scared self.

An animal, worn out, on the verge of giving up.
The malady I carry has no speakable name. Only a distant
drumming,
A doorbell ringing on my forehead and I cannot answer
For I don't know who's entering nor what may fall out.

Still, I find strength at the tip of my toes, a sort of leverage
Making me a daily version of Lazarus, lifting from the dead of
the night,
From the soundless bottom of the well from which I recoil
constantly.

The ghouls, dressed in doctor's garb, release my puzzled
screams.
How could I convalesce and still actively abandon myself?
How could I leave and yet remain in the same body and life?
What do I abandon and what do I keep?

I am the exception to every medicine book.
My body knows no rules, only a battle,
Only the scar-covered mantle in which I chase life.

And when I find her, when I set eyes on her, I'm a hunter.

I'm the ever-growing tiger, with such hunger, that not even
Angels from the skies nor the devils from Tartarus could
fulfil.
Life has been running from me, leaving my fingers throbbing
With storms of new blood.
But now she's staring me in the eye. She surrenders.
Life owes me a great deal and I'm about to require it.

SOUR

I squeeze the lemon in my palm,
The juice rapes my wounds and still
It burns less than the stinging inside of my heart,
And its zest holds less acidity than my head.

If I could be a little more sweet than bitter,
Maybe I could find the tight space between
What happiness should be, and what they make it seem to be,
Maybe I could understand the right way to shed my skin,
Maybe its thickness could be rebuilt.

But I become so undone whenever the toll squeezes me,
Asking for a bribe, for its mandatory dimes.
It won't let me trespass until I'm sour enough,
And I cannot sugar-coat it this time.

I dance with the acids of my stomach.
They climb my throat like a scream that never blows.
I'm scavenging for an alkaline smile,
That brings the colours back to this hepatic system.

SORE

I wait, longingly, for this that has no designation.

Like a child, on the tip of her toes, leaning on the fence,
Searching for this carriage that never comes.
I force my vision until it hurts, trying to look further,
If someone appears at the corner, even if slowly approaching.

I don't know how I got here.

If abandoned as an orphan on a bleak street or if I stranded
From a pleasant group of people that did not understand my
longing,
This missing part of me, because they had a name for it
And I had another.

But the road seems to grow ever longer, never letting me pick
a handful
Of soil to read the tracks of those before me.
I just sit and wait patiently for some frail meaning to come to
life,
For an old professor to stop by and take the time to explain
the meaning of my existence.
I had a bag of crumbs to make it easier to come back, but I
became eager,
Hungry for everything, so I ate my path to the core.

Only a raw strip of land connects me to the moment,
Both feverish, both red, both boiling with anxiety.

I am a timeless goer, following whatever seems more

promising
To find the answers.
When I sleep, beneath the open sky, mistaking fireflies for
stars,
My dreams almost let me catch a glimpse. They give me
scenery,
They give me colours, they give me voice.
But as a punishment for waking, it all melts away; like dirty
snow just after winter
My head aches with the attempt to remember.
It hurts so much that, when I'm sleeping, I can hear the
secrets of life,
But when I try to repeat them, the memories go silent as
gossipers do .
They just stare and I feel unwelcome.

Maybe I'm greedy, unpleased with peacefulness.
I want more. I want life to take me by her arms and tell me
With bold, uppercase letters, THE TRUTH.

I want her to feed me Honesty's porridge until I can't
swallow.
Overfed and underslept, I want life to tell me how I got here,
Who walked this road before me, with me,
And how we met.

Only waiting for the earth to unfold; the mushroom cloud is
not enough.
I want to ride the explosion, the violent chariot of life,
Consuming the peripherals until they become one.

I want to conduct it to where I want to go,

Not knowing the limitations of life, time, and physics,
Of nothing that could ever stop us.

Make life sore and exhausted by the multitude of questions
It will have to answer until we both fall,
Satisfied and wise, understanding frantically
Each draught of air we consume.

UNWORTHY

I drain like puddles, back to where I've been.
The same dark pit, slowly wetting the stairs,
Leaving behind little droplets of dissatisfaction
And lost expectations.

I'm the only one to blame.

The carvings on the walls are all mine,
And the bloodstains
From my grated fingers are fruits of my own inflictions,
For I have a vain wish to believe in much
More than my hands can bare.

In my attempts to retrieve from the walls what
They never promised to give, I find myself
Repeatedly punching the rough texture,
Donating all that composes me in hope
That the walls will become a door for me to escape.

In my mind, the cave will soften and rebuilt
Into a grand portal to receive whatever is left of me.

It will mend my open wounds, stitch my cravings
By the fireplace as we rant about how long it took
For life to align our way.

My hands dismantle as flowers, giving up,
Disgorging their petals to the ground.

And my body curls down as a lonely stalk would,

After losing its purpose, staring at the soil where,
Not long ago, it was a promising seed.

As always, expectation took the best of me.

My roots have been easy-going from the start.
Never really doubting the earth, hurling to the centre
With hunger and blind faith.
Love was my fertilizer and I'd bloom as fast as I could
Just to get my fix.

But love ends.

Fields dry and catch on fire,
So weary even a warm breath could become a hazard.
The only difference is how long we can water it,
Which, by myself, I cannot for long.

So I dry up.

As always, expectation took the best of me.

STASIS

I'm in suspension.
My head and feet float,
Even my eyes cannot lock onto anything.

I hold cement in my hands,
But it doesn't make me sink.

The city carries on and I'm in slow motion,
Trying to hold on to it,
To the moment,
To whatever it is that lingers by the corner,
Whenever the dots are close to connection
We're drifted, divided and splintered.
I'm torn apart.
You're behind the ceiling lights,
The way the rays dissolve through my sight.
You're behind the paint strokes on the wall,
And I cannot catch a grasp of you.

I'm comatose,
Living below the turning of the clock,
Hearing the calls of somewhere I'm not from,
And it almost feels I could go back home
But I'm still,
My body remains in a full cast and impotent,
The anorexic veil derides me,
If I stare at it too much,
You'll be looking at me.
I revolve in bed, feverish,
Drenching the sheets and my clothes.

My bones hurt as if the flesh would fall off.
It feels like time is getting its portion of me.

But I cannot move,
And I wouldn't move without you,
So we'll just remain,
Senselessly listening to each other's bray.

DEFENCE

The black holes I left behind seemed to contain you.
I saw myself free of charges and free of labels,
Crying with my lungs, raw, until they emptied and filled with
renewal.
I believed, with all my strength, I had left you behind.

Years passed unharmed, only the occasional trembling by the
sound
Of the syllables of your name and the way they resonate in a
crowded room,
The way heads turn to find the origin as if conditioned to
find you,
Or at least that is how I felt, at least that's how you sounded.

My strong carcass began to cave in, cracking with each verse
and every
Bit of history I could collect, scrambled amidst a whole
universe of fantasy,
Lies and untold truths they've covered you with, more of a
character and less
Of a person, less a part of who I used to be.

But if I could clear the clouds, scrap the crust with an
incommensurate will,
I'd find the beauty of those afternoons when you were you
and you knew me.

I've been inundated by you, soaked in every graft of skin
available,

Wearing you as a life jacket as you push me up and down the
water.
I'll never know what scares me the most-- your presence or
absence.
We're in the fluid and every raindrop is a memory I'd try to
collect if I wasn't
Trying so hard to keep myself above the sea.

Drowning is the common sense of our lineage, giving in,
closing our eyes
For a long denied eternity.
Crows and doves fly and die just the same, the flip of a wing
is the span of life.
You didn't change it for me but I'd do my best to change it
for us.

Linger up there for me, for this unproclaimed poetry.
I may never be as great, *but I may be just as brave to forbid
Our past selves to fade into oblivion.*

ABSENCE

Absence. That is what I don't want.

The silence you leave in the walls when you leave
Through the door.
It is as if the plaster knew how to mock me by reverberating
you,
By making me believe you're still in the room,
Only to remind me of the space between my body and yours.

Everything learns to stretch when someone is missed.

Hours take their time to pass and clocks are mere plates,
That serve nothing but the *cold meal of long distance.*

I could swear the wind has been searching for you,
The way it enters, rampantly, shaking the windows to their
bones,
But exits before I have a chance to breathe it in.
It is not me that it wants.

I've been stepping into voids.

The longing inside me devours the environment
And forgives nothing.

No sign of reality, no vegetation.

Wherever I go, I take the emptiness of the universe with me.
The stars exploding into headaches in attempts to create
Your presence again.

They demand you back.
Planets weight on my back because they lost their orbit,
The way your black hair would sustain them,
Keeping them afloat as a hanging mobile.

Absence hurts as deep as hunger, the whole body ravaged by
cramps,
Pleading for what it does not receive,
And blaming me for not running fast enough to reach you,
And bring you back to where you should be.

So please, help me stay in one piece and return,
As fast as this absence hurts, as fast as the wind freezes me.

Return fast so that this becomes a diluted bad dream,
From which I'll wake up, as if you had never left.

THE ART

I've taken pieces out of me to fill the frame.

It is colossal, oppressive, and intensively golden.

Like a cathedral or any sacred ground that stands above lies.
I've collected material from my insides,
Still warm and steamy.

At first, they were easy to catch,
Smooth to remove and almost painless to detach.
They seemed to have a precise place and they'd glue perfectly.
The frame was—dare I say—,
Almost beautiful.

Then, one day, bits of flesh fell off from the display,
Small and relatively unnoticeable.
Only a strong observer would, after a good examination,
Realize that maybe those missing spots were not intentional.

I dug deeper.

The new pieces were thicker and harder to grasp.
They came out surrounded by a strip of pain.
I gulped them down and they accepted the frame.

It was filled again, some parts a better fit than others,
But a respectable work of art to hang on the wall
Of the less perceptive and less vigilant.

Yet one morning, that began like any other,
The frame fell wholly to the ground.
I woke by the sound of its heaviness and disregard.

I looked inside and the remains were so scarce and so
internal,
They could barely fill a reproduction from a gift shop.
Determined, I reached once more and the broken pieces hurt,
violently.
They were slippery and retreated,
They had absolutely no will to partake in reconstruction.

And I tried to convince them as I convinced myself
That the frame was worth filling,
That the museum was worth maintaining,
That the passers-by would be touched by it enough to
examine it,
And that their examination was worth the pain,
And worth the removal of so many pieces
To fill the frame.

As I sat there, gluing together the threadbare slices of what
remained,
I saw the river of red ink flowing, unaware the drain was
sipping it as I cleaned and bleached the frame,
Over and over again.

Then the paint seemed much more compelling to my deflated
body,
More resourceful, more cooperative.

The frame sat stained at the corner as I carefully removed my
skin,
And inch by inch by inch
I filled it with permanent poetry.

STRAYED

I do not belong.

This feeling of not being part,
Of not quite fitting in,
Follows me around as a crooked toy,
Mocking my own crooked existence,
As if I was broken or misplaced.

A bee that discovered the flower to be a better home
Than the hive.
The kind of honey I produce is too bitter,
Or maybe theirs is too sweet for my palate
And I need astringency.

The bloodline coagulates and does not flow as free as it used
to.

It stagnates and, as all the rest,
I become bloated into purple tones.
I vocalize a never-ending asthma because the words do not
leave,
Only guilt and repulse, only the desire for a new place,
A new address, a new body.

I have no postal code and even my fingerprints are frail.
Somehow, they know I'm not meant to be identified here,
That I don't want to leave any shards behind,
Not even a shallow memory that might linger in one's mind,
Because, perhaps if I dispose of this strayed version of

myself,
I could bear the light of who I really am.

Or at least, who I'm supposed to be.

I AM AFRAID

I am afraid.

This is the line I've used the most in my life.
This is my script, given to me at birth.
My tagline, the name I go by more than my own.

I am afraid.
I am afraid.

I am fear.

Fear in the shape of a person, fear with a thick skin,
And hair that changes more than the weather in my town.
My town made me afraid of so many things,
It made turning corners safely seem like the lottery,
It made crossing the street a ludicrous game;
Going to the market a round of Russian Roulette.

Bullets hitting the red tomatoes and bell peppers,
And perhaps me, in the middle of it, a salad of fear,
Seasoned with the tears of residual panic.

Fear is the wrinkled shirt I have on, and never remove.

It smells.
Fear has such a strong body odour,
It does not weight, at first. It does not bother.
It is good, some say, it is preventive.
Fear has prevented me from being happy for years,
Fear has prevented me

From everything.

I am afraid.

The monsters left the underground of my bed;
They own houses, they drive cars,
They walk around shopping futilities for their homes.
I am afraid they might see me petrified;
Reminisce on terrifying me further.
I'll laugh out of terror,
I'll be the subject of the night.

I am afraid and it is the feeling I know best.
I am afraid and it is the feeling I'm best known by.
When I shake hands, the whole world shakes with me.

My fearful eyes remove the blankets that keep people safe,
A mirrored image of their broken plaster saints,
I am so afraid, people have become fearful of me.

I am so afraid, I am fear.

THE POPPIES HAVE DRIED

The poppies have dried.
Their red petals lost the colour
And faded into something ill.

A wound half-healed,
Half-pungent,
Wide open but painless.

A childhood trauma one learns to live with.

It is autumn again.

But not brought about by the good path of descending.
Not the golden trail of old leaves.
Not the fresh air of renewal.
Only the stale odour of delay,
Of being stuck.

I feel like a seed willing to grow way beyond my size.

But blocked. Starving and withering,
Discovering the cruelty of the world way too soon.
Born where flowers are plucked and torn and stepped over.

I used to be strong as a rock, useful as an ochre brick.

Water would find its way around me instead of punching my
back.

I would raise places above the river, I'd keep files and people safe.

But it seems I've become malleable, far too much,
Allowing water to tear me apart, to rip out of me the signs of
strength,
And the river I once defeated is now my biggest fear.
I wake up fighting for air as if foreseeing
The water attempting to drown me,
Before I learn how to breathe
Under it.

The poppies have dried.

The blood red of my heart has dried.

It maintains its shape but cannot be touched,
Like the oldest artwork you can think of,
Hanging from a dull wall, adored by thousands,
But loved by no one.

COLD STONE

I wish your cold stone had
A postcode engraved on it.
That my words could be protected
From the rain and the accidents
That unsheltered written words often meet.

I wish that the post office would reach further.
About seven feet beyond their daily effort,
To deliver pieces of me to you;
Send remnants back, stained in red ink
With all of your corrections,
Telling me where to go,
What to avoid,
But mostly I'm certain you'd advise me
To be bold and daring.

Even though I know the answers to my internal questions,
There's a lack of motivation,
And long cobwebs sewed by fear.
My hands seem to move slower than before,
Though doctors cannot find an explanation.
They don't understand what kind of vitamin I lack.

I try to force my hands to work.
The pile of paper just grows before me,
But fear grows just as tall.

"Have the guts", you'd say.

We'd scream motivational sentences across the room,

Wrap each one in a rhyme or metaphor,
To pretend the poem was not born out of pain.
To pretend it doesn't hurt to have only
The frail security of a blank paper.
To pretend it doesn't hurt to feel lonely
Inside our own minds.

I wish your cold stone had a vacancy,
So I could find a place to call home
That would not be as frightening as this open coffin.

There is more life and oxygen in the corners of your bones
Than I'm able to breathe, up here.
I wish I could find the same peaceful blanket of dirt
Where I wouldn't have to think of anything more,
And nothing more would be asked of me.

MOVING OUT

The orange sun seems to be at war with me,
Pushing light into my crescent lids still in love with the
darkness.

I wish it would let me sleep until fairness grows from the tip
of my numb fingers, spreading roots over the mattress.
Until my body becomes a beacon of spring.
This is not a one-day job.

The world depletes me.

Mankind has reaped all the fruits I bore
And I don't want to raise myself from the bed.
I want to remain where dreams and I speak the same old
language.
Where the only villains are the ticking of the clock, and the
cold that invades the seams of my blanket.

**I want nothing more than the steadiness of a violent
change.**

The peacefulness of a one-way ticket to another land that
wouldn't be found.
I want to be carried away by the burning smoke of a train,
that leads me
To places you'll never be, places where no one knows my
name.
To leave in the middle of the night without traces. You'd ask
yourself

If I was ever real or the fragment of a dream that lingers.

I want to erase my existence and create a new one, where I'm
rediscovered
And respected as a rare subject on display.

The limpid carcass reminding people that nothing ever ends.

Because I don't want to vanish from the world but to vanish
from you,
To deceive the claws you call hands and the sun you call eyes.

I want to stray in streets I cannot pronounce,
And my tongue will call each and every avenue
"Freedom."

PATTI

Books choose us.

Our movements towards the shelves are merely ceremonial.

We believe to be the ones making a decision,
And that's enough for the egotistical mind.
But books are the ones to choose.
The right ones, for the right moment,
Like prophets.

Patti has been talking for weeks inside my head.

Refusing change while embracing it, the tornados,
The destroyed shelters, the abandoned dreams.
The things we lost and found, only to lose again
When we wake up.

Only to forget again.
To find our hands empty, the nails almost piercing the skin
In such hunger to retain.
But somethings are ought to be lost.

They vanish so that we find ourselves in the process.

Or at least so we don't lose ourselves.
They make the sacrifice.

I storm out of the coffee shop
As if I'm running from a great predator.

It is my mind I'm running from,
Afraid some ordinary scene might catch my attention
And the poem, still fragile, will be but a memory.

A fading Polaroid picture
Forgotten in the sun,
Until I'm left with only a cut-out in monochrome.

I feel more protected with books against my torso,
An armour announcing to the world who I am.

People pay no attention to women holding books,
And that's the kind of protection I want.
Yet I feel juvenile, holding them against my chest,
As if I'm again hiding, pretending I'm not here,
Until people forget me.

I'm not used to admiring the living,
So I look at the chair in front of me and lift my empty glass
As if she could see it.

As if it was enough to thank someone
By pouring a string of black coffee.

I exchange words for more words. And a few tears to remind
me that
Some sentences need a pause.
I raise my glass to thank the ones alive inside the pages, but
lost
Everywhere else.
Writers I know.
Writers I love.

Writers I never heard of before,
Now I carry some affection inside me.

I lost an earring during the same chapter she lost her black
coat.

Both old, used, perhaps cheap. Both infused with happenings.

We mourn lost things. We mourn that no amount of belief
Can bring some things back, not entirely.
You can never read a book for the first time again, you can
never
Feel the same emotions
Each word will be absorbed only once.
Each new author will make their presentation only once.
Then you're acquaintances, then friends. Sometimes enemies.
Sometimes lovers.
A mother and her child.
Or two dying comrades breathing into each other's noses.

Sometimes you cannot finish a book,
Because you cannot follow its lesson.
You're not ready.

I have books I may never finish. I've made my peace with it.
Others have changed me completely.
As a tornado that shakes an entire landscape.
I'm left with my structures hurt, but still standing,
A colossal Alamo bravely fighting the wind
That turns the pages of my own life book.

OUROBOROS

Hands pop out of my eyes,
Trying to pull me inwards.
I want to unsee time.
To reverse my knowledge into blind blissfulness.

There are holes appearing in my arms
As if I was burning from the inside,
And they seem to consume everything.

To undo whatever they approach,
To unravel everything into words.
A book inverted.
The dictionary of my existence.
Everything I have ever seen or touched or been
Catalogued from the end to the beginning.

From the cold earth around my grave
To the red walls of the womb,
Which end up being the same thing,
With a slightly different temperature.
But the familiar silent agony of not knowing what to expect
Nor whom to be next.

Every word I have ever said
Turns into thousands of random poems.
I've lost my solid nature,
And my steadiness.
All that remains is voice,
Rushed voice,
Curling before my tongue as the eye of a snail

Refusing to look straight into the root of the pain.

Before I fully awaken, I visit a room.
Three doors encircle me.
The oppressive dark wood seems to be in a hurry.
Time has a physical form here.
A 60-minute chair stares at me,
Its velvet eyes call as those of a wild cat in rest,
Who wins over the prey through the lure,
Instead of violence.
I could sit my life away,
Or at least what remains.

But the furniture screams decision.

One of the doors must be opened
And the person I'll cross to be is a ghost.

Perhaps they won't close their eyes to the future,
Won't give in to the hands that pull and pull like the ocean.

Perhaps they'll destroy every record of the past
And move forward, only forward.
The heart steady as a compass.
Or perhaps they'll find a moment worth waiting for.

As I accept the sounds of the past
And turn the knob to the future,
I sign off my departure as a delayed plane.

I have no space for overloaded baggage
Nor can I remain on the ground.

I erase the itinerary so that every place is a new one,
And every landscape has the chance of capturing my heart
one more time.
The world dissolves into newness and I reach for it
With the curiosity of a child,
But the eyes of a sage.

DISCLAIMER

Some of the poems presented here have been published first in online magazines. However, the versions here have been edited, updated and/or rewritten.

My thank you to the magazines who have been the first houses for my works.

All pictures by Giulia de Gregorio Listo

ABOUT THE AUTHOR

Giulia de Gregorio Listo is a Brazilian poet. Her work has appeared in worldwide publications such as The Ibis Head Review, Literati Magazine, Literally Literary, The Junction and others.

She is fascinated by the multitude of feelings one can experience, and by how everything is a reflex of the universe, over and over again. She hopes her poems will help to reveal a bit of the light and shadow dance that composes life.

Follow her on social media:

 @giulia_listo

 @giulialistopoetry

You can find more of her work on www.giulialisto.com
For further inquiries, contact her on giulialisto@gmail.com

Made in the USA
Middletown, DE
14 May 2023